30 DAYS OF PRAYERS AND DECLARATIONS TO
RELEASE THE DAY & RECLAIM INTIMACY WITH GOD

CYRIL OPOKU

Command Your Evening: *30 Days of Prayers and Declarations to Release the Day and Reclaim Intimacy with God*

© 2025 Cyril Opoku. *PrayerScripts*. All rights reserved.

No part of this publication may be reproduced, stored in a retrieval system, or transmitted in any form or by any means—electronic, mechanical, photocopy, recording, or otherwise—without the prior written permission of the publisher, except in the case of brief quotations used in reviews, articles, or devotionals.

Published by *Quest Publications*

ISBN: 978-1-988439-66-2

Cover design by *Quest Publications (questpublications@outlook.com)*

Unless otherwise indicated, all Scripture quotations are taken from the World English Bible (WEB), which is in the public domain. For more information, visit: www.worldenglish.bible

This book is a work of devotional encouragement. It is not intended to replace biblical study, pastoral counsel, or professional therapy.

Printed in the United States of America.

First Edition: July 2025

For more books like this, visit **PrayerScripts:** *https://prayerscripts.org*

Contents

Contents .... *iii*
Preface .... *x*
Introduction .... *xii*
How to Use This Book .... *xv*

DAY 1 1
Laying Down the Weight 1
Strength for the Next Stretch 2
Eyes Back on the Kingdom 3
Raising Ruins Into Glory 4
Stillness for the Soul 5

DAY 2 7
I Cast It All on You 7
Transform My Inner World 8
Set My Mind on Things Above 9
The Hand of God Is With Me 10
Learning to Live Light 11

DAY 3 13
I Lay It All Down 13
Made New From Within 14
Eyes Fixed on Jesus 15
Restorer of Broken Places 16
The Gift of His Presence 17

DAY 4 18
I Will Not Be Afraid 18
Create in Me Again 19
Let My Gaze Be Straight 20

You Are Rebuilding Me 21
Peace Beyond Understanding 22

DAY 5 23
Trading Anxiety for Peace 23
Washed and Renewed by Mercy 24
Light for the Path Ahead 25
Restoring What Was Broken 26
God Gives Rest as a Gift 27

DAY 6 28
Letting Go to Run Free 28
Renewed in the Spirit of My Mind 29
Eyes Forward, Heart Ahead 30
You Will Raise Me Again 31
Entering the Rest of Faith 32

DAY 7 33
Letting Go for the New 33
A Fresh Wind of Revival 34
Perfect Peace in a Steady Mind 35
Restored and Strengthened Again 36
Peace Will Be My Dwelling 37

DAY 8 38
I Confess and I Am Free 38
New Mercies, New Strength 39
Meditation that Moves Me Forward 40
Reclaiming What Was Ruined 41
Come Away and Be Refreshed 42

DAY 9 43
- I Let It Go 43
- Clothed in the New Nature 44
- Setting My Mind on Life 45
- Double for My Trouble 46
- Dwelling in the Shadow of God 47

DAY 10 48
- Forgiveness Frees My Soul 48
- Victory Breathes New Strength 49
- Taking Every Thought Captive 50
- Called Back to Purpose 51
- Safe Sleep, Secure Heart 52

DAY 11 54
- Mercy Has the Final Say 54
- Soaring Again with New Strength 55
- Teach Me to See Again 56
- Prisoner of Hope No More 57
- I Wait in Quiet Confidence 58

DAY 12 59
- Burdens Lifted, Blessings Received 59
- You Satisfy My Soul Again 60
- Wisdom for the Way Forward 61
- Joy Rising from the Ruins 62
- Resting in Grace-Filled Spaces 63

DAY 13 64
- Letting Go to Trust Again 64
- Guided and Watered Again 65
- Choosing What Really Matters 66

Healing in the Rising Light ... 67
The Breaker of Bondage ... 68

DAY 14 ... 69
I Lay Down Weakness ... 69
Revived and Raised Again ... 70
Delight in His Direction ... 71
You Have Not Abandoned Me ... 72
Silent Trust, Steady Peace ... 73

DAY 15 ... 74
He Hears and Delivers ... 74
Anchored in Unshakable Hope ... 75
My Labor Is Not in Vain ... 76
From Rubble to Precious Stones ... 77
Peace Be with Me ... 78

DAY 16 ... 79
Free From Guilt and Shame ... 79
God's Not Finished With Me ... 80
Fix My Hope Fully ... 81
Healing the Land Within ... 82
My Heart Is at Peace ... 83

DAY 17 ... 84
I Am Free Indeed ... 84
He's Making All Things New ... 85
Eyes Enlightened with Hope ... 86
The Lord Roars Over Me ... 87
Rest from the Labor, Not the Purpose ... 88

DAY 18 89
Bring My Soul Out 89
I Have Power, Love, and Peace 90
Set My Heart to Seek 91
Speak Life to My Dry Places 92
Be Still and Know 93

DAY 19 94
You Heard My Cry 94
Fresh Oil for the Evening 95
I Will Not Be Shaken 96
Glory After This 97
Every Promise Fulfilled 98

DAY 20 99
Freedom for the Wounded Places 99
Your Word Revives Me 100
I Commit and Align 101
Restore Me, O God 102
I Enter Peace, Not Pressure 103

DAY 21 104
Out of Distress, Into Space 104
Restoring the Years 105
Approved and Equipped 106
Now Is the Appointed Time 107
Blessed in the Finished Work 108

DAY 22 109
Beauty for My Ashes 109
Born Again to a Living Hope 110
Seek and Return 111

Redemption Has a Name 112
He Never Sleeps—So I Can 113

DAY 23 114
Safe in the Day of Trouble 114
Double for My Shame 115
Seek with All My Heart 116
Restore My Soul 117
You Will Lie Down Secure 118

DAY 24 119
Sung Over with Love 119
Revived by Truth 120
Turn My Eyes from Vanity 121
The Desert Will Bloom Again 122
Strength and Peace Are Mine 123

DAY 25 124
He Heals the Broken Places 124
A New Heart Within Me 125
Remain in Me 126
Healing and Restoration Declared 127
Held by the Hand of God 128

DAY 26 129
Where the Spirit Is, I'm Free 129
Overflow with Hope 130
Do Not Love the World 131
From Lame to a Remnant 132
Peace from the God of Peace 133

DAY 27 134
Let Go, Stand Still 134
Satisfy Me Again, O God 135
Keep the Fire Burning 136
Joy Will Be Restored 137
Covered in Blessing and Peace 138

DAY 28 140
Letting Go, Trusting the Plan 140
Strengthened by Everlasting Comfort 141
Let Your Love Lead Me 142
Arise Again by His Word 143
Taste and See His Peace 144

DAY 29 145
Fear Has No Hold Here 145
Quiet Confidence Will Rise Again 146
The End Is Better 147
Be Restored, Be Made Whole 148
Grace for This Day Only 149

DAY 30 150
Letting Go of Vengeance 150
Fullness of Joy Again 151
Open the Door of My Heart 152
Tears Will Not Be Wasted 153
Kept From Falling 154

Epilogue *155*
Encourage Others with Your Story *157*
More from PrayerScripts *158*

Preface

> Let my prayer be set before you like incense; the lifting up of my hands like the evening sacrifice.
> —Psalms 141:2 WEB

There's a sacred stillness that descends as the day begins to fade. In that in-between space—after the work is done, before the night begins—we are offered a divine invitation: to pause, release, and realign. *Command Your Evening* was born out of this invitation.

"May my prayer be set before You like incense; may the lifting up of my hands be like the evening sacrifice." (Psalm 141:2)

This book is the third in the **"Command Your Destiny"** prayer series, following *Command Your Morning* and *Command Your Night*. While the morning is for activating your day and the night for sealing your rest, the evening holds a unique, often overlooked purpose. It is the moment to surrender what has been, to receive God's presence afresh, and to posture your heart for renewal and reflection. It is not the start or the end—it is the holy middle. And that space matters deeply to God.

In *Command Your Evening*, you'll journey through 30 days of intentional, Spirit-led prayers and prophetic declarations centered around five key evening themes: **Release, Renew, Refocus, Rebuild, and Rest**. Each day is anchored in Scripture and designed to help you let go of the weight of the day, receive God's perspective, and experience His peace, power, and presence.

Whether you're coming home from a full day of labor or closing a quiet afternoon of waiting, these prayers will help you transition with purpose. You'll find strength to forgive, clarity to realign your focus, courage to rebuild what was shaken, and serenity to enter your night in the embrace of God.

Let this not just be a book you read, but a rhythm you live. As you command your evening, may your prayers rise like incense, and may the God who never sleeps meet you with mercy, renewal, and perfect peace.

In Christ's authority,
Cyril O.
Illinois, July 2025

Introduction

What if the way you ended your day could change the way you live it tomorrow? There is a battle over every transition—and evening is one of the most spiritually neglected.

As the sun sets and the day winds down, many feel the pull to disconnect—mentally, emotionally, and spiritually. But this is not the time to grow numb or drift aimlessly through the evening hours. In heaven's rhythm, the evening is not just a wind-down—it's a window. A sacred hour where destinies are recalibrated, burdens are lifted, and hearts are re-centered in the presence of God. This is the moment to reset with intention, recalibrate your focus, and realign with God. Every evening is a sacred threshold—a time to release the burdens of the day, renew your spirit, refocus your priorities, rebuild what life may have broken, and rest in the unwavering presence of your Father.

Command Your Evening is the third book in the **Command Your Destiny** series—following *Command Your Morning* and *Command Your Night*. While the morning is a launching pad and the night a final seal, the evening stands as a threshold—a divine pause to release the day and receive God's perspective before the night fully settles in.

Command Your Evening is not just a devotional—it is a prophetic tool, a declaration of faith, and a weapon of spiritual readiness to help you reclaim the in-between hours, when the work has paused but the warfare has not. Through Scripture-based prayer and intentional engagement with God, your evening becomes a stronghold of peace, power, and preparation.

Each of the 30 daily prayers in this book is built on five Spirit-led themes that mirror the flow of God's evening invitation:

- **Release** – Let go of the weight, the regret, the warfare, and the noise of the day. Release what you cannot fix and surrender it to the One who holds it all.
- **Renew** – Invite the refreshing wind of the Spirit to renew your strength, your purpose, your thoughts, and your emotional clarity.
- **Refocus** – Realign your attention with heaven. Clear the clutter of distraction and recenter your mind on eternal priorities.
- **Rebuild** – Allow God to restore and rebuild what was broken, delayed, or lost in the hours behind you. Speak life to ruins and hope to what seems halted.
- **Rest** – Not just physical rest, but deep, soul-level restoration in God's presence—where peace anchors you and His nearness becomes your shelter.

Every evening holds power. It is the space between action and rest, between striving and stillness, between your doing and God's renewing. What you do in this space matters. It determines whether you carry the day's weight into your sleep or lay it at the feet of the One who never slumbers.

You were not meant to stumble through your evenings in weariness or worry. You were called to command them—through prayer, through presence, and through prophetic alignment. Let this rhythm continue in your life. Let every sunset be a reminder that

God is not done working, speaking, or moving. The evening still belongs to Him—and so do you.

So take your place. Speak your prayers. Declare His promises.

And command your evening.

How to Use This Book

This book is designed to guide you into a powerful, intentional, and Spirit-led evening rhythm. Each of the 30 days offers five prophetic prayer segments, each built around a specific theme that aligns with the flow of God's evening invitation: **Release, Renew, Refocus, Rebuild,** and **Rest.**

Here's how to engage each evening:

1. **Set the Atmosphere**: Find a quiet space, away from distractions. If possible, light a candle, play soft worship music, or simply sit in stillness before the Lord. Make this time sacred.

2. **Read the Scripture for Each Theme**: Each day is anchored in five carefully selected Scriptures—one for each theme. You can read them all at once or meditate on them one at a time as you move through the prayers.

3. **Pray Each Section Out Loud**: The prayers are written in the first person so you can speak them as your own. Declare them boldly, slowly, and with faith. These are not passive recitations—they are prophetic utterances rooted in God's Word.

4. **Pause and Listen**: After each prayer, take a moment to pause and invite the Holy Spirit to speak to your heart. Journaling what you hear can deepen your evening encounter.

5. **Repeat or Linger**: If a certain theme (like Release or Refocus) especially resonates with what you faced that day, linger there. The goal is not to rush, but to receive.

6. **Do This for 30 Evenings**: Go through the book day by day, but don't feel pressured to finish in exactly 30 days. Let it be led by grace. Some days may invite deeper reflection or repetition.

This is more than a routine—it's a divine exchange. Each evening, you are releasing what burdens you, receiving what God longs to give, and preparing your spirit for the night ahead.

Let your voice rise. Let heaven hear.

Command your evening.

DAY 1

RELEASE

LAYING DOWN THE WEIGHT

> Cast your burden on Yahweh, and he will sustain you. He will never allow the righteous to be moved.
> —Psalms 55:22 WEB

I boldly release the burdens of this day at Your feet, O Lord. I refuse to carry what You never intended for me to hold. Every anxious thought, every lingering frustration, every unresolved tension—I lay it down. You are my burden-bearer, my steady anchor, my Deliverer in the chaos of life. I trust You with what I can't fix, and I surrender what I can't control. I release the weight of expectations, deadlines, misunderstandings, and unspoken wounds. I release it all, right here, right now.

Father, I come to You because You care deeply for me. Your Word assures me that when I cast my cares upon You, I am not ignored—I am held. You invite me to drop every heavy thing and trust You to uphold me. I am not crushed, I am not overwhelmed, and I am not alone. You sustain me. You strengthen me. And You surround me with peace that the world can't take away. I choose freedom over pressure. I choose peace over panic.

I walk into my evening lightened and lifted. I have nothing to prove, and nothing to hide. I give You what I cannot carry, and I thank You for exchanging it with Your strength. I'm not just releasing stress—

I'm releasing control, and choosing trust. My hands are open. My heart is light. My soul is at rest.

In Jesus' name, Amen.

Renew

STRENGTH FOR THE NEXT STRETCH

> But those who wait for Yahweh will renew their strength. They will mount up with wings like eagles. They will run, and not be weary. They will walk, and not faint.
> —Isaiah 40:31 WEB

Lord, I come to You this evening asking for divine renewal. The day has drawn out of me energy, time, emotion—and I need to be filled again. I will not try to keep running on yesterday's strength. I wait on You now, knowing that those who wait upon You are lifted, empowered, and refreshed. You are my endless source. You don't run out. You don't grow tired. You are the One who strengthens the weary—and I open myself to receive from You.

Father, I need fresh endurance—not just for the body, but for the mind and spirit. I surrender the worn-out places in me. Where discouragement lingers, breathe hope. Where apathy hides, stir desire. Where fatigue sits, pour vitality. I refuse to let the pace of life drain the purpose out of my soul. Let Your Spirit breathe fresh fire into me—fire to believe again, to serve again, to dream again. You promised to renew my strength, and I take You at Your word.

This evening, I trade weariness for wings. I trade striving for stillness. I trade frustration for faith. You are reviving me—not just to survive, but to rise. I declare that this evening marks a turning point. My strength is being renewed like the eagle's. I'm being lifted above every drag and delay. I run and do not grow weary. I walk and do not faint.

In Jesus' name, Amen.

Refocus

Eyes Back on the Kingdom

> But seek first God's Kingdom, and his righteousness; and all these things will be given to you as well.
> —Matthew 6:33 WEB

Father, in this moment of stillness, I pause to refocus my heart on what truly matters. The day has tried to scatter my attention, dilute my passion, and cloud my purpose—but I choose now to realign. I lift my eyes off distractions, off the pressures, off the noise—and I fix my gaze on You. Let the clutter fall away. Let Your kingdom come into full view again.

I seek first Your Kingdom and Your righteousness. I refuse to be pulled in a thousand directions by things that have no eternal value. I don't want to merely do good things—I want to do the God-things You've prepared for me. So realign my desires, O Lord. Reset my priorities. Let my evening be governed not by what's urgent, but by what's holy. If I've lost sight of what You're doing, help me see again. Show me where You're at work—and let me join You.

I declare that my focus is clear and sharp. My heart is fully Yours. I am anchored in the eternal, not tossed by the temporary. You are my center, my compass, my true North. This evening, I seek Your presence over performance, and Your will over my wandering. I'm locked in again. And I won't let go.

In Jesus' name, Amen.

Rebuild

Raising Ruins Into Glory

> In that day I will raise up the tent of David who is fallen, and close up its breaches, and I will raise up its ruins, and I will build it as in the days of old; that they may possess the remnant of Edom, and all the nations who are called by my name," says Yahweh who does this.
> —Amos 9:11-12 WEB

Father, I thank You that You are the God who rebuilds what is broken. Where others see rubble, You see revival. Where life has fallen apart, You speak life into the ruins. This evening, I stand in agreement with Your plan to restore, to renew, and to raise up what has been torn down. I surrender every broken place in my life—whether relationships, dreams, confidence, or calling—and I invite You to begin the rebuilding process.

You are the Master Builder, and nothing is too shattered for You to redeem. I don't come to You in despair—I come in hope. Because You don't just repair what was lost, You restore it in greater measure. You are reviving dead places. You are redeeming lost time. You are turning ashes into beauty and making what was barren fruitful again. What the enemy tried to destroy, You are turning into a testimony of grace.

This evening, I partner with Your restoration. I declare that the days of desolation are ending, and a new foundation is being laid. Walls of peace, gates of praise, and paths of purpose are being built anew. I will not mourn over what's missing—I will rejoice in what You're rebuilding.

In Jesus' name, Amen.

Rest

Stillness for the Soul

> In peace I will both lay myself down and sleep, for you, Yahweh alone, make me live in safety.
> —Psalms 4:8 WEB

Lord, I choose to rest—not just physically, but emotionally, mentally, and spiritually. I lay aside the weight of striving, overthinking, and emotional exhaustion. You are my peace. You are my hiding place. You are my still waters in a chaotic world. Even now, I lean into Your presence where my soul can exhale. I may not have every answer, but I trust the One who holds it all together.

Father, You invite me into soul-rest, not performance. You teach me that peace is not found in the absence of problems, but in the presence of Your nearness. You quiet every internal storm with a single word. I take refuge in You this evening—not to escape reality, but to receive perspective. You silence the noise within me, and settle my heart like a child weaned and safe. I refuse to live tense and burdened. I am resting in You.

I declare that this evening is marked by inner stillness. I release every mental loop, every unresolved emotion, every unnecessary weight. Your peace is not temporary—it's sustaining. I'm not shaken. I'm not scattered. I am centered in Your grace and covered by Your presence. In the quiet, You restore me. In the calm, You reframe me. I rest in You, and You alone.

In Jesus' name, Amen.

DAY 2

RELEASE

I Cast It All on You

> Casting all your worries on him, because he cares for you.
> —1 Peter 5:7 WEB

I boldly release every burden into Your hands, Lord. I was not created to carry what only You can hold. The weight of the day, the pressure of responsibility, the stress of decisions and delays—all of it, I cast on You. I will not entertain anxiety. I will not hold on to fear. I refuse to live bowed down by emotional heaviness or spiritual unrest. You are my Father, and You care deeply for me. So I let go—freely and fully.

I cast every silent concern, every invisible wound, every unsaid worry. I lay before You the things I cannot fix and the outcomes I cannot control. I won't pretend to be strong when You are offering to be my strength. I choose the peace that comes from surrender. I acknowledge that You are sovereign over my circumstances and merciful in Your dealings with me. You don't dismiss my pain, but You invite me to give it to You—and so I do.

I walk into this evening with open hands and a light heart. I have released it all. I am unburdened. I am unchained. My soul is free from the grip of worry because I know You hold it all together. I trust You, Lord—not just with my future, but with this very moment.

In Jesus' name, Amen.

Renew

TRANSFORM MY INNER WORLD

> Don't be conformed to this world, but be transformed by the renewing of your mind, so that you may prove what is the good, well-pleasing, and perfect will of God.
> —Romans 12:2 WEB

Lord, as this day winds down, I open myself to the renewing power of Your Spirit. The world has tried to conform my thoughts, steal my joy, and dull my fire—but I resist the pattern of this age. Instead, I lean into Your perfect will for me. I seek transformation, not behavior modification. I want to be changed from the inside out. So this evening, I invite You to do a deep work within me.

Renew my mind, Lord. Cleanse me from toxic thoughts, limiting beliefs, and unholy agreements I've made in my heart. Uproot every lie that has taken residence in my mind today. Wash over me with truth, and awaken my spiritual senses. Let my thoughts reflect the mind of Christ—bold, clear, peaceful, and aligned with Your Word. I don't want to be defined by how the world sees me, but by who You say I am.

As I step into the evening hours, let fresh strength rise in me. Refresh my outlook. Rekindle my vision. Let joy replace exhaustion and clarity replace confusion. I declare that I am being renewed even now—transformed by truth and revived by grace. The world will not shape me. You will.

In Jesus' name, Amen.

Refocus

SET MY MIND ON THINGS ABOVE

> If then you were raised together with Christ, seek the things that are above, where Christ is, seated on the right hand of God. Set your mind on the things that are above, not on the things that are on the earth.
> —Colossians 3:1-2 WEB

Father, I lift my eyes higher. I shift my gaze away from what went wrong, what I didn't finish, and what still feels out of place. I choose to fix my thoughts on what is eternal, not what is urgent. My mind is not a playground for distraction—it is a sanctuary for truth. I set my affections on things above, where Christ is seated in victory. I focus not on the noise, but on the voice of the One who reigns.

I repent for the moments today when I gave my attention to things that didn't deserve my energy. I turn away from small thinking, emotional clutter, and shallow pursuits. I realign with heaven's perspective. Let my heart be drawn to what pleases You. Let my decisions, my reflections, and even my conversations this evening flow from a place of Kingdom alignment.

I declare that my vision is being corrected. I see through the lens of eternity. My thoughts are lifted, my emotions are anchored, and my goals are clarified. I will not be pulled into distractions or discouraged by what is temporary. My eyes are fixed. My spirit is focused. My heart is full of heaven.

In Jesus' name, Amen.

REBUILD

THE HAND OF GOD IS WITH ME

> Then I answered them, and said to them, "The God of heaven will prosper us. Therefore we, his servants, will arise and build; but you have no portion, nor right, nor memorial, in Jerusalem."
> —Nehemiah 2:20 WEB

Lord, I thank You that You are the God who builds, and You are building with me. What the enemy tried to break today, You are already restoring. What was delayed, You are setting in motion. I declare with boldness: the hand of my God is with me. I do not face brokenness alone. You are not just watching—You are working. And You are giving me strength to rebuild what I thought was lost.

You see the places where confidence cracked, where faith wavered, where progress slowed. But You have not abandoned the project of my life. You are still the Architect, still the Master Builder. You will strengthen my hands to finish what You started. I believe that every setback is becoming a setup for greater testimony. You will empower me to rebuild my vision, my hope, my purpose, and my peace.

So this evening, I lift my head. I will not mourn over the rubble—I will rise and rebuild by Your Spirit. What looked impossible this morning is already being touched by Your hand. I rejoice not in what I see, but in what You've promised. The work is Yours. The victory is Yours. And You have chosen to do it with me.

In Jesus' name, Amen.

Rest

Learning to Live Light

> Take my yoke upon you, and learn from me, for I am gentle and humble in heart; and you will find rest for your souls. For my yoke is easy, and my burden is light."
> —Matthew 11:29-30 WEB

Jesus, You are my rest. Not just for my body, but for my soul. I come to You now—not in striving or struggle—but in surrender. You invite me to take Your yoke and learn from You. I lay aside the burdens of performance and the false weights I was never meant to carry. I open my heart to the rhythm of grace. Teach me how to live light, how to walk free, and how to move at heaven's pace.

This evening, I release the pressure to do more, be more, fix more. I receive Your gentleness instead. I embrace the unforced rhythms of grace. Let my emotions settle in Your truth. Let my thoughts slow down and align with Your peace. I don't have to figure everything out this evening. I don't have to fight every battle. I can rest—mentally, emotionally, spiritually—because You are my refuge and my teacher.

I declare that I am no longer a prisoner to pressure. I am no longer driven by fear or perfectionism. I am grounded in grace and growing in rest. This evening, I make a holy exchange—my heaviness for Your lightness, my chaos for Your calm. I walk in rhythm with You.

In Jesus' name, Amen.

DAY 3

RELEASE

I Lay It All Down

> "Come to me, all you who labor and are heavily burdened, and I will give you rest.
> —Matthew 11:28 WEB

I come to You this evening, Jesus, with full confidence in Your invitation to bring my weariness to You. I'm not hiding my exhaustion—I'm handing it over. I refuse to carry the weight of emotional fatigue, spiritual heaviness, or unresolved pressure from this day. I lay it all down. I choose not to manage it—I surrender it. You are my resting place, and in You, I find freedom from every burden I've been holding too tightly.

This evening, I release the strain of performance, the anxiety of outcomes, and the ache of things left undone. You never asked me to carry it alone. You never intended for me to be crushed under the load of life. So I come to You—not to vent, not to numb, but to exchange heaviness for Your presence. You are my strong tower and my gentle Shepherd, and I yield to Your care.

I declare that I am stepping into peace. I am letting go of everything that drains me and holding fast to the One who restores me. The burdens of this day will not follow me into this evening. I walk forward with lightness, clarity, and the joy of surrender. In Jesus' name, Amen.

Renew

Made New From Within

> Therefore we don't faint, but though our outward man is decaying, yet our inward man is renewed day by day.
> —2 Corinthians 4:16 WEB

Lord, this evening I welcome Your renewing power into every corner of my soul. I may feel worn on the outside, but I know You are at work in my inner being. While the day may have drained my strength, You are renewing me from within. My spirit is not growing old—my spirit is being refreshed. Even when my body is tired, Your Spirit in me is alive, active, and strong.

You are restoring vitality where weariness tried to settle. You are pouring in joy where discouragement crept in. I don't have to conjure strength—I receive it from You. I don't need to strive for resilience—I tap into the well that never runs dry. You are the God who renews day by day, breath by breath, moment by moment.

So I speak life over myself this evening. I am not diminishing—I am being renewed. I am not fading—I am being refilled. My strength is rising. My heart is lifted. My soul is anchored. I am not surviving this day—I am being revived through it. What fades in the natural is being made new in the Spirit.

In Jesus' name, Amen.

Refocus

Eyes Fixed on Jesus

> looking to Jesus, the author and perfecter of faith, who for the joy that was set before him endured the cross, despising its shame, and has sat down at the right hand of the throne of God.
> —Hebrews 12:2 WEB

Jesus, this evening I choose to fix my eyes on You. The day may have pulled my attention in many directions, but I realign now with the only focus that matters—You, the Author and Finisher of my faith. You are my center. You are my clarity. You endured the cross for joy—and that same joy is available to sustain me. I look away from what distracted me today and fix my eyes on the One who endured it all.

Where I allowed frustration, fear, or comparison to cloud my vision—cleanse my focus. Help me to see again with spiritual eyes. Let me remember what truly matters. Let me live for Your applause, not the world's approval. Let the cross be my compass and eternity be my lens. Strip away the noise and center me in Your purpose once more.

I declare that my eyes are set. My spirit is steady. My gaze is clear. I am not tossed by today's emotions or blurred by its challenges. I am rooted in truth and fixed on grace. Jesus, You are the goal. You are the standard. You are my joy—and I will not look away.

In Jesus' name, Amen.

Rebuild

Restorer of Broken Places

> Those who shall be of you shall build the old waste places; you shall raise up the foundations of many generations; and you shall be called Repairer of the Breach, Restorer of Paths with Dwellings.
> —Isaiah 58:12 WEB

Lord, I thank You that You are not only the God who creates but the God who rebuilds. This evening, I come to You with the broken moments of my day—the misunderstandings, the setbacks, the disappointments—and I lay them before You. You are the One who restores ruins and raises foundations. You see beyond what's cracked. You see potential where others see loss.

Where something in me was shaken today, rebuild it. Where a wall was breached—be it trust, confidence, or clarity—mend it. You promised to raise up ancient ruins and restore paths to dwell in. I choose not to live in the rubble. I choose to stand in faith, believing that You are already at work restoring what was harmed.

This evening, I align my heart with Your blueprint. Rebuild my resolve. Reinforce my peace. Renew the places that felt abandoned or weak. You are the Master Restorer, and what You touch, You make stronger than before. I won't mourn over what's lost—I will rejoice in what You're reviving.

In Jesus' name, Amen.

Rest

The Gift of His Presence

> He said, "My presence will go with you, and I will give you rest."
> —Exodus 33:14 WEB

Father, I welcome Your presence this evening. I don't need a vacation to find rest—I need You. You promised that Your presence would go with me and give me rest, and I receive that now—not just for my body, but for my mind and emotions. I don't need to strive to be okay. I simply need to abide. You are my rest—not just a moment of peace, but the Person who gives it.

I rest from internal battles—the questions I can't answer, the feelings I can't name, the expectations I didn't meet. I step into the calm of being known and loved by You. In Your presence, I don't have to earn peace—I encounter it. You are not rushing me. You are not pressuring me. You are inviting me to breathe, to be still, to know You are near.

I declare that my inner world is coming into rest. I am not driven by deadlines or defined by performance. I am safe. I am held. I am resting in the assurance that You are with me and that is enough. Your presence is my pause. Your nearness is my relief. I rest, deeply and wholly, in You.

In Jesus' name, Amen.

DAY 4

RELEASE

I WILL NOT BE AFRAID

> Don't you be afraid, for I am with you. Don't be dismayed, for I am your God. I will strengthen you. Yes, I will help you. Yes, I will uphold you with the right hand of my righteousness.
> —Isaiah 41:10 WEB

This evening, I release fear, anxiety, and intimidation into Your hands, Father. I will not be dismayed by the demands of this day or the challenges that lie ahead. You are with me. You are my strength. You are the One who upholds me with Your righteous right hand. I refuse to carry fear into the evening. I will not let uncertainty write the script for my soul. I let go of every trembling thought, every whispered doubt, and every shadow of fear.

You are my Defender, my ever-present help, my strong support. Even when I felt weak today, You never left me. Even in the moments where I faltered, You stood firm. So I release the pressure to be perfect, and I take hold of Your promise to sustain me. I surrender the fear of failure, the fear of people's opinions, and the fear of "what if." You are greater than them all.

I declare that fear has no grip on me. I am not dismayed. I am not shaken. I am not alone. You are my confidence and my covering. I rest this evening in the truth that I am held, I am helped, and I am upheld. In Jesus' name, Amen.

RENEW

CREATE IN ME AGAIN

> Create in me a clean heart, O God. Renew a right spirit within me.
> —Psalms 51:10 WEB

Lord, I bring my heart before You this evening—not to cover it up, but to let You do what only You can do. I ask You to create in me a clean heart and renew a steadfast spirit within me. I don't want to just feel better—I want to be made new. I don't want to carry old residue into new moments. So I invite Your Spirit to do a deep cleansing work inside of me.

Wash away the grime of the day—every careless word, every hidden motive, every misplaced desire. I don't want a patch-up job. I want a renewal. Purify me, Lord. Take what has grown weary or calloused and make it tender again. Let Your Spirit breathe fresh life into dry places and restore the joy of my salvation.

I declare that I am being renewed—not from the outside in, but from the inside out. My heart is becoming whole again. My spirit is becoming steady again. I am not stuck in cycles of shame or discouragement. I am being made new by mercy, strengthened by grace, and restored by the love of a holy God. In Jesus' name, Amen.

Refocus

Let My Gaze Be Straight

> Let your eyes look straight ahead. Fix your gaze directly before you. Make the path of your feet level. Let all of your ways be established. Don't turn to the right hand nor to the left. Remove your foot from evil.
> —Proverbs 4:25-27 WEB

Father, this evening I choose to refocus my mind and set my gaze straight ahead. I turn my eyes away from distractions—those subtle things that pulled me off course today. I fix my vision on Your truth. I fix my purpose on the path You've marked out for me. I ask for spiritual clarity to see what matters most and courage to walk in it.

I guard my heart from detours and unnecessary battles. I align my steps with wisdom and my decisions with purpose. Where I've been tempted to swerve or stray, realign me. Let me not turn to the right or the left, but stay steady on the narrow road You've prepared. Keep my focus clean. Keep my motive pure. Keep my pace in step with You.

I declare that my focus is clear. I will not be pulled by comparison, slowed by confusion, or hindered by fear. I am locked in, looking forward, and led by Your Spirit. What's behind me will not define me. What's before me will not distract me. I will walk the path of life with undivided vision.

In Jesus' name, Amen.

Rebuild

You Are Rebuilding Me

> I will build you again, and you will be built, O virgin of Israel. You will again be adorned with your tambourines, and will go out in the dances of those who make merry.
> —Jeremiah 31:4 WEB

Lord, I thank You that even when I feel scattered, You are rebuilding me. This evening, I surrender every place in me that has been torn down by the day—by stress, criticism, failure, or pain. You are the God who rebuilds—not only circumstances, but souls. You are restoring me, shaping me, and calling me beautiful again.

Where I've felt worn out, You are refreshing me. Where joy has cracked, You are repairing it. Where my voice felt silenced, You are giving me song again. Like a faithful builder, You take the pieces and form something stronger than before. You are not done with me. You haven't discarded me. You are building something eternal within me—even through the days that feel unproductive or painful.

I declare that I am under divine reconstruction. What life tried to tear down, You are raising up. What the enemy tried to distort, You are realigning. I am not broken beyond repair. I am a testimony in progress. I see Your hand restoring me, piece by piece, breath by breath.

In Jesus' name, Amen.

Rest

Peace Beyond Understanding

> And the peace of God, which surpasses all understanding, will guard your hearts and your thoughts in Christ Jesus.
> —Philippians 4:7 WEB

Lord, I enter this evening wrapped in Your peace. Not the fragile peace the world offers—but the kind that transcends all understanding. I quiet my thoughts and surrender my emotions under the shelter of Your presence. You guard my heart and mind with a peace that holds me steady, even when things around me are uncertain.

I don't need everything to make sense to rest in You. I don't need every problem solved to breathe deeply. You are the God who gives peace as a Person, not just a feeling. You are near, and that is enough. I refuse to be anxious over what's next. I choose the stillness that comes from knowing You are already in tomorrow.

I declare that peace is reigning over my mind this evening. Confusion is silenced. Restlessness is calmed. Doubt is dismantled. You are my still point in a spinning world. I rest not because the world is quiet, but because my spirit is grounded in the One who never changes.

In Jesus' name, Amen.

DAY 5

RELEASE

TRADING ANXIETY FOR PEACE

> In nothing be anxious, but in everything, by prayer and petition with thanksgiving, let your requests be made known to God. And the peace of God, which surpasses all understanding, will guard your hearts and your thoughts in Christ Jesus.
> —Philippians 4:6-7 WEB

Father, I come before You this evening with open hands and an open heart. I release every anxious thought, every restless emotion, and every unspoken worry into Your capable hands. I will not be weighed down by uncertainty or fear. I bring every concern—spoken and unspoken—into Your presence through prayer and thanksgiving. I choose to trust, not to tremble.

Thank You for being a God who listens. Thank You for caring about the details of my life. I release the stress of the day: the unfinished tasks, the miscommunications, the unexpected detours. I don't need to carry it—I only need to surrender it. I offer my gratitude as a sacrifice and let Your peace guard my heart and mind like a shield.

I declare that peace surrounds me now—not peace rooted in circumstances, but in Christ. My heart is anchored. My mind is quiet. Anxiety has no room to live here. I will not be pulled into panic. I will be led by peace. I am free from fear, and filled with trust. In Jesus' name, Amen.

Renew

Washed and Renewed by Mercy

> Not by works of righteousness which we did ourselves, but according to his mercy, he saved us through the washing of regeneration and renewing by the Holy Spirit,
> —Titus 3:5 WEB

Lord, as this evening unfolds, I come not in my own righteousness, but covered by Your mercy. I thank You that I am not renewed by works, but by the washing and regeneration of Your Spirit. You cleanse what I cannot fix. You renew what I cannot repair. You restore what I didn't even realize was broken. It's not my effort—it's Your mercy.

I yield to the renewing work of Your Spirit. Let Your grace soak into every dry place. Where shame lingered, wash me clean. Where discouragement tried to take root, uproot it with joy. You are making me new—not just on the surface, but at the core. Your Spirit is breathing life into places that felt dead, stagnant, or numb.

I declare that I am a new creation in Christ—not once, but continually being renewed day by day. I am not who I was. I am not who I feared I would become. I am who You say I am—cleansed, chosen, and made whole by mercy. I rise from this day's weariness with fresh strength, fresh purpose, and a renewed spirit. In Jesus' name, Amen.

REFOCUS

LIGHT FOR THE PATH AHEAD

> Your word is a lamp to my feet, and a light for my path.
> —Psalms 119:105 WEB

Father, this evening I pause to refocus. The day may have blurred my vision or dimmed my passion, but I realign now with Your Word, which is a lamp to my feet and a light to my path. You are not leading me in confusion. You are leading me in clarity. Your Word cuts through the fog of distraction and reveals the next step with divine precision.

I choose to follow Your light instead of leaning on my own understanding. Let every decision, every conversation, and every thought this evening be filtered through the truth of Your Word. I don't need all the answers right now—I only need to follow the light I've been given. And in that light, I find peace.

I declare that I am not wandering. I am being guided. I am not aimless. I am being led. Your Word is my compass. Your truth is my anchor. I am walking with purpose, because I am walking in Your light. No shadow can hide the path You've prepared for me.

In Jesus' name, Amen.

Rebuild

Restoring What Was Broken

> 'After these things I will return. I will again build the tabernacle of David, which has fallen. I will again build its ruins. I will set it up,
> —Acts 15:16 WEB

Lord, I thank You that You are not only a God of beginnings, but a God of restoration. You see what has fallen, and You promise to raise it up. This evening, I invite You to rebuild the parts of my life that have been worn down by time, pressure, or pain. Restore what was lost. Reclaim what was damaged. Revive what seemed dead.

You said You would rebuild what has collapsed, and I believe You are doing that now. Whether it's vision, relationships, hope, or inner strength, You are restoring me from the inside out. You don't just patch up—I see You laying fresh foundation. You are making the ruins beautiful again.

I declare that rebuilding is already in motion. Heaven's hand is upon my life. The broken places are not the end of my story—they are the soil for a stronger future. I rise from discouragement with faith that restoration is my portion. You are not finished with me. You are just getting started.

In Jesus' name, Amen.

REST

GOD GIVES REST AS A GIFT

> It is vain for you to rise up early, to stay up late, eating the bread of toil; for he gives sleep to his loved ones.
> —Psalms 127:2 WEB

This evening, Lord, I receive the rest that only You can give. Not just sleep, but true soul rest. You give it to Your beloved, not as a reward for striving, but as a gift of love. I do not have to earn Your peace—I simply receive it. I cease from striving. I release the lie that productivity equals worth. I embrace the truth that Your presence is my portion.

I rest in knowing that I am fully known, fully loved, and fully held. I do not have to finish everything to be at peace. You are already at work, even when I pause. You give rest not because I am weak—but because You are kind. I let go of mental noise, emotional pressure, and spiritual tension. I rest in the shadow of Your wings.

I declare that this evening is holy ground. My rest is not a delay—it's a divine reset. You give me rest, and I receive it with joy. I lay down the weight, and I pick up Your peace. I am not restless. I am restored.

In Jesus' name, Amen.

DAY 6

RELEASE

LETTING GO TO RUN FREE

> Therefore let's also, seeing we are surrounded by so great a cloud of witnesses, lay aside every weight and the sin which so easily entangles us, and let's run with perseverance the race that is set before us,
> —Hebrews 12:1 WEB

Lord, this evening I release every weight and sin that clings so closely. I will not carry baggage into the next moment of my life. I lay down the burdens that have slowed me down—unforgiveness, regret, self-doubt, fear, and distraction. I refuse to live tangled in things You've already given me grace to overcome. I let go so I can run free.

I release the need to explain myself, to prove myself, or to compare myself. I fix my eyes forward. I fix my eyes on Jesus. I release the emotional clutter, the mental loops, the spiritual stagnancy—and I press into the liberty You've given me. The race is still set before me, and I will run it with perseverance, not with pressure.

I declare that this evening marks a divine shedding. I am not bound by what I once carried. I am not stuck in what once slowed me. I am free to move forward with focus, with faith, and with fire. Nothing old will cling to me. I run unhindered. In Jesus' name, Amen.

Renew

Renewed in the Spirit of My Mind

> and that you be renewed in the spirit of your mind,
> —Ephesians 4:23 WEB

Father, this evening I open myself to be renewed in the spirit of my mind. I don't want to merely change behavior—I want transformation from within. I invite You to renew the way I think, the way I feel, and the way I process this day. Where my thoughts have grown weary or jaded, pour fresh truth. Where my attitudes have soured, infuse them with grace.

I strip off the old mindset and embrace the new. I reject patterns of negativity, defeat, and fear. I welcome the mind of Christ—clear, courageous, compassionate. I don't have to be stuck in the thoughts of yesterday. You are doing a new work, and it starts in my mind. Align my internal world with heaven's reality.

I declare that I am being renewed right now. Not tomorrow—now. Your Spirit is rewiring my perspective, refreshing my thinking, and reshaping my outlook. I will not leave this day the same way I entered it. I am transformed by truth, and empowered by renewal.

In Jesus' name, Amen.

REFOCUS

EYES FORWARD, HEART AHEAD

> Brothers, I don't regard myself as yet having taken hold, but one thing I do. Forgetting the things which are behind, and stretching forward to the things which are before, I press on toward the goal for the prize of the high calling of God in Christ Jesus.
> —Philippians 3:13-14 WEB

Jesus, this evening I turn my eyes from what is behind and stretch toward what lies ahead. I forget the failures of today, the frustrations of the past, and the distractions that tried to pull me away. I fix my focus on the upward call—on Your purpose, Your prize, and Your presence. I will not rehearse what's already behind me. I will reach forward.

Where my thoughts wandered today, bring them back. Where I've been discouraged by slow progress, remind me of the joy that's still before me. Let passion replace regret. Let vision replace discouragement. I am not stuck in what was—I'm stepping into what will be. The prize is too great, and the calling is too real, for me to look back now.

I declare that my focus is sharp, my heart is steady, and my eyes are locked on destiny. I forget what I must forget. I remember what I must pursue. I am reaching, running, and pressing toward everything You've promised.

In Jesus' name, Amen.

Rebuild

You Will Raise Me Again

> You, who have shown us many and bitter troubles, you will let me live. You will bring us up again from the depths of the earth. Increase my honor, and comfort me again.
> —Psalms 71:20-21 WEB

Lord, this evening I come to You with every place in me that has faced hardship, disappointment, or loss. I thank You that though I've seen trouble, You promise to revive me again. You are the God who restores my soul and lifts me up from deep places. You will increase my greatness and comfort me on every side.

You are not finished with me. You saw the low valleys, but You are raising me to new heights. You allowed the shaking, but You're using it as a foundation for strength. You are rebuilding the places in me that felt diminished. You are restoring the dreams I thought were buried. You are comforting me not with temporary relief, but with lasting peace.

I declare that what seemed like the end is becoming the beginning. The broken places are being rebuilt into testimonies. I rise with renewed purpose, enlarged vision, and fresh hope. The pain of the past will not define the architecture of my future. You are raising me up—for Your glory.

In Jesus' name, Amen.

Rest

Entering the Rest of Faith

> There remains therefore a Sabbath rest for the people of God. For he who has entered into his rest has himself also rested from his works, as God did from his.
> —Hebrews 4:9-10 WEB

Father, this evening I step into the rest that only faith provides. You said there remains a rest for the people of God—and I claim that rest now. Not because my work is done, but because I trust in what You've already done. I lay down the pressure to fix, to finish, and to figure it all out. I trust in Your finished work, not my frantic work.

I enter into rest by surrendering control. I quiet the inner critic, the anxious planner, the voice of unrest that says I must do more. You are my Rest, not my reward. You welcome me into stillness, not as punishment but as provision. I find calm in Your care and stillness in Your sovereignty.

I declare that I am resting—not because life is easy, but because You are faithful. I don't need to earn peace; I live in it. I cease from striving. I receive divine stillness. I rest not in circumstance, but in covenant. This is the rest of faith—and I enter it gladly.

In Jesus' name, Amen.

DAY 7

Release

Letting Go for the New

"Don't remember the former things, and don't consider the things of old. Behold, I will do a new thing. It springs out now. Don't you know it? I will even make a way in the wilderness, and rivers in the desert.
—Isaiah 43:18-19 WEB

Lord, this evening I release the past into Your hands. I refuse to be imprisoned by what was when You are doing something new. I let go of yesterday's regrets, missed opportunities, old pain, and old patterns. I will not allow memories to hold my spirit hostage. I lay them all down so I can make room for the new thing You are springing up in my life.

I release stale thinking, small expectations, and the lingering weight of "what could have been." I trust that You are making rivers in my desert and roads in my wilderness. You are the God of the impossible, and I will not limit You by clinging to the past. My eyes are open to the fresh work You are doing, even now.

I declare that I am not defined by what I've lost or what I've gone through. I am being prepared for something new. I will not look back—I look forward with faith and with joy. The old has passed. The new has come. I release and I receive. In Jesus' name, Amen.

Renew

A Fresh Wind of Revival

> "Repent therefore, and turn again, that your sins may be blotted out, so that there may come times of refreshing from the presence of the Lord,
> —Acts 3:19 WEB

Father, I turn to You this evening for renewal—not just of strength, but of spirit. You said that when we return to You, times of refreshing will come from Your presence. So here I am, returning. I repent of going through this day without full dependence on You. I repent for dullness of heart and for anything that has numbed my passion for You.

Now breathe on me, Lord. Let the winds of refreshing revive my soul. Let joy return where weariness had crept in. Let hope rise where discouragement had lingered. I don't want to go through the motions—I want to live in the overflow. I ask You to stir up my love for You and renew my fire for Your purpose.

I declare that I am being refreshed in the presence of the Lord. My dry places are being watered. My spirit is being revived. I feel the turning. I sense the shift. This is not the end—this is renewal, rebirth, and revival. I receive it fully.

In Jesus' name, Amen.

REFOCUS

PERFECT PEACE IN A STEADY MIND

> You will keep whoever's mind is steadfast in perfect peace, because he trusts in you.
> —Isaiah 26:3 WEB

Lord, this evening I realign my focus and fix my mind on You. I refuse to be ruled by anxious thoughts, scattered emotions, or what-ifs. You promise perfect peace to the one whose mind is stayed on You. So I anchor my mind—not in circumstances, not in outcomes, but in Your unchanging truth.

Where I've been distracted today, draw me back. Where my thoughts have wandered, center me again. You are my Source. You are my Confidence. When I set my mind on You, fear dissolves and clarity returns. I am not swayed by every emotion or burdened by every outcome. I stand firm because my focus is firm.

I declare that peace floods my inner world. My mind is not a battleground—it is a sanctuary. My thoughts are aligned with heaven. I choose to dwell on Your faithfulness, not my fears. I choose truth over turmoil. And in that choice, I find rest.

In Jesus' name, Amen.

Rebuild

Restored and Strengthened Again

> But may the God of all grace, who called you to his eternal glory by Christ Jesus, after you have suffered a little while, perfect, establish, strengthen, and settle you.
> —1 Peter 5:10 WEB

Father, I thank You that even after I've suffered or struggled, You Yourself promise to restore, confirm, strengthen, and establish me. This evening, I place every broken place in Your hands. I trust You to rebuild me—not in my strength, but in Yours. I will not stay in sorrow. I will not sit in defeat. You are lifting me up and strengthening me again.

You are the God who restores dignity, confidence, vision, and courage. Where the day left me feeling undone, You are putting me back together stronger. You're not just mending cracks—you are laying a firm foundation under my feet. I'm not just getting through this—I'm being rebuilt for greater.

I declare that this is not the end of the story. I am being established in purpose. I am being strengthened in grace. You are shaping me for something greater. And what I've lost in the fire, You are restoring in power. I will rise again—not by my might, but by Your Spirit.

In Jesus' name, Amen.

Rest

Peace Will Be My Dwelling

> The work of righteousness will be peace; and the effect of righteousness, quietness and confidence forever. My people will live in a peaceful habitation, in safe dwellings, and in quiet resting places.
> —Isaiah 32:17-18 WEB

Lord, I step into the evening with full assurance that Your peace is my portion. Not a temporary escape, but a permanent dwelling. You promised that the effect of righteousness is peace, and the result of righteousness is quietness and confidence forever. I rest in that this evening—not because life is perfect, but because I am planted in Your presence.

I embrace the peace that settles deep within. It is not the absence of conflict, but the presence of Your rule in my heart. I don't just want a peaceful moment—I want a peaceful lifestyle, a peaceful spirit, a peaceful home. Let Your peace reign over every area of my life.

I declare that I will dwell in peace. My mind is quiet, my spirit is settled, my atmosphere is governed by Your presence. Nothing missing, nothing broken. Peace is not a wish—it is my reality because I walk in step with You. And in this divine peace, I rest.

In Jesus' name, Amen.

DAY 8

Release

I Confess and I Am Free

> I acknowledged my sin to you. I didn't hide my iniquity. I said, I will confess my transgressions to Yahweh, and you forgave the iniquity of my sin. Selah.
> —Psalms 32:5 WEB

Father, this evening I come before You not with pretense, but with honesty. I lay bare my heart. I confess where I have missed the mark today—in thought, in word, in action, and in motive. I'm not hiding anything from You. I acknowledge my sin and shortcomings, and I thank You for the promise of forgiveness and freedom.

I refuse to carry guilt into the night. I release the weight of silence, the burden of shame, and the heaviness of unspoken failure. You are faithful to forgive. You cover me with mercy. You cleanse me and call me righteous—not because I am perfect, but because You are. I confess, and I am cleansed. I repent, and I am restored.

I declare that I am walking into this evening free. I am not bound by condemnation. I am not defined by my faults. I am a child of God—clean, forgiven, and restored to fellowship. The joy of salvation is mine again. The relief of release is mine this evening.

In Jesus' name, Amen.

RENEW

NEW MERCIES, NEW STRENGTH

> It is because of Yahweh's loving kindnesses that we are not consumed, because his compassion doesn't fail. They are new every morning. Great is your faithfulness.
> —Lamentations 3:22-23 WEB

Lord, this evening I rest in the mercy that meets me every single day. I thank You that even when the day felt long, when I stumbled or struggled, Your compassions never failed. They are new every morning—and I receive them fresh this evening. Your faithfulness is my anchor and my hope.

I welcome Your mercy like rain on dry ground. I let go of yesterday's shame and today's strain. I soak in the grace that revives and renews. You do not deal with me according to my weakness, but according to Your love. So I lean into that love now and let it wash over every weary place in me.

I declare that I am being renewed right now—not because I earned it, but because You are faithful. I am not stuck in the old—I am rising in the new. Your mercies have the final word. Your love rewrites my story daily. I breathe deep, I receive fully, and I stand renewed in the light of Your unfailing love.

In Jesus' name, Amen.

Refocus

Meditation That Moves Me Forward

> This book of the law shall not depart from your mouth, but you shall meditate on it day and night, that you may observe to do according to all that is written in it; for then you shall make your way prosperous, and then you shall have good success.
> —Joshua 1:8 WEB

Father, this evening I recalibrate my focus by centering my heart on Your Word. I choose not to dwell on the distractions or disappointments of the day. Instead, I meditate on Your promises. I rehearse Your truth. I realign with what You've spoken, because that is where true success and clarity are found.

Let Your Word be my compass. Let it stir my faith, shape my thoughts, and direct my next steps. I don't want to just read it—I want it to read me. I want to think on it, speak it, and live it. I turn away from the noise of the world and tune in to the whisper of heaven.

I declare that as I meditate on Your Word, I gain insight, direction, and peace. I will walk into the rest of this evening with clarity. My mind is not scattered—it is focused. My heart is not restless—it is planted in truth. I move forward, not in my own wisdom, but in divine instruction.

In Jesus' name, Amen.

Rebuild

Reclaiming What Was Ruined

> They will rebuild the old ruins. They will raise up the places long devastated. They will repair the ruined cities, that have been devastated for many generations.
> —Isaiah 61:4 WEB

Lord, You are the Restorer of places long devastated, and this evening I invite You to rebuild what has been broken in my life. Whether by my own actions or by the harshness of life, I bring to You every ruined place—dreams delayed, hope deferred, confidence shaken, joy diminished. You are the God who rebuilds ancient ruins, and You are doing it in me.

You don't just restore buildings—you restore hearts. You rebuild identity. You reestablish purpose. I give You the broken bricks of my day and ask You to make something beautiful with them. Where others see waste, You see the foundation for a testimony. I trust Your process and Your timing.

I declare that ruins are becoming restoration. That what was torn down will rise up stronger than before. You are replanting joy, reviving strength, and rebuilding my life from the ground up. This is not the end—this is divine construction. I believe it, and I receive it.

In Jesus' name, Amen.

Rest

Come Away and Be Refreshed

> He said to them, "You come apart into a deserted place, and rest awhile." For there were many coming and going, and they had no leisure so much as to eat.
> —Mark 6:31 WEB

Jesus, You called Your disciples to come away and rest, and this evening, I answer that call. I come away—not in body only, but in spirit. I pull away from the noise, the pressure, and the busyness of the day to be with You. You are not only my Savior; You are my Sanctuary. In You, I find refreshing that no schedule or vacation can provide.

You invite me into rest—not as an escape, but as a reset. I rest in Your presence. I rest in Your finished work. I rest knowing I don't have to prove anything. I don't have to perform. I just need to be still and be near. You refill what life drains. You restore what duty depletes.

I declare that this evening, I will be refreshed. My heart will be light. My mind will be clear. My soul will be calm. I am not striving—I am sitting at the feet of the One who restores all things. This is holy rest, and I enter into it with joy.

In Jesus' name, Amen.

DAY 9

Release

I Let It Go

> Let all bitterness, wrath, anger, outcry, and slander, be put away from you, with all malice. And be kind to one another, tender hearted, forgiving each other, just as God also in Christ forgave you.
> —Ephesians 4:31-32 WEB

Father, this evening I make a holy decision: I release bitterness, wrath, anger, and every grudge I've carried today. I will not let offense linger in my spirit or poison my peace. I refuse to rehearse conversations that hurt me or replay actions that offended me. Instead, I choose to forgive. I choose compassion. I choose mercy.

You have forgiven me of so much, and I will not withhold that same grace from others. I release not just the person, but the pain. I let go of the wound, the weight, and the words. I choose love over resentment. I choose peace over payback. This is not weakness—this is freedom. And I walk into my evening with a clean heart and open hands.

I declare that I am not bound by bitterness. I am full of mercy. I am free from offense. I am walking in the Spirit and releasing every root of resentment. I am covered by grace and I extend that grace. What tried to cling to me today is being shaken off in the presence of God. In Jesus' name, Amen.

RENEW

CLOTHED IN THE NEW NATURE

> Don't lie to one another, seeing that you have put off the old man with his doings, and have put on the new man, who is being renewed in knowledge after the image of his Creator,
> —Colossians 3:9-10 WEB

Lord, this evening I take off the old self—the attitudes, mindsets, and behaviors that don't reflect who I am in You. I strip off comparison, insecurity, pride, and frustration. I lay down anything that does not look like Christ. I don't want to carry the old me into the future You've prepared for me.

Now I put on the new self—created in Your image, shaped by Your Spirit, and fueled by Your love. I choose compassion. I choose humility. I choose joy. I am not the sum of my mistakes or the echo of my past. I am being renewed day by day in knowledge and power, becoming more like You.

I declare that I am being renewed in my identity. My nature is not bound to who I used to be. I am being shaped into the likeness of Christ. Every part of me—mind, emotions, character—is being transformed. I put on the new, and I walk in newness.

In Jesus' name, Amen.

Refocus

Setting My Mind on Life

> For those who live according to the flesh set their minds on the things of the flesh, but those who live according to the Spirit, the things of the Spirit. For the mind of the flesh is death, but the mind of the Spirit is life and peace;
> —Romans 8:5-6 WEB

Father, this evening I bring my thoughts into alignment with Your Spirit. I choose not to set my mind on the things of the flesh—on worry, offense, or self-centered desires—but on the things of the Spirit. I fix my attention on what brings life and peace. I silence the internal noise and tune into Your still, small voice.

I refuse to let my mind wander into fear or frustration. I center myself in Your Word. I focus on truth, on eternity, on grace, on what is good and pure. I recognize that my mindset determines my direction—and I choose the path of peace. Let every anxious or carnal thought be replaced with divine perspective.

I declare that my mind is clear. My spirit is calm. My focus is steady. I think thoughts that lead to life. I set my mind on the Spirit, and in doing so, I enter a deeper place of peace and purpose. I walk forward with clarity.

In Jesus' name, Amen.

Rebuild

Double for My Trouble

> Yahweh turned the captivity of Job, when he prayed for his friends. Yahweh gave Job twice as much as he had before.
> —Job 42:10 WEB

Lord, You are the God who restores, and this evening I thank You for what You're rebuilding in me. Just like Job, You saw my losses, my pain, and my prayers—and You are turning the story. You are giving double for the trouble. You are restoring relationships, joy, favor, and hope. What the enemy meant for evil, You are reversing for good.

You are not just giving back what was taken—You are increasing it. Where there was brokenness, You are building beauty. Where there was delay, You are bringing acceleration. You don't just heal wounds—You bring restoration and redemption. I trust You with what I cannot fix. I trust You to make it better than it ever was.

I declare that this is a rebuilding season. Heaven is answering with overflow. I will not live in lack. I will not remain in grief. I will rejoice in what's being rebuilt. You are restoring my life, and I will testify.

In Jesus' name, Amen.

Rest

Dwelling in the Shadow of God

> He who dwells in the secret place of the Most High will rest in the shadow of the Almighty.
> —Psalms 91:1 WEB

Father, I come into the evening seeking not just relief, but refuge. I dwell in the secret place of the Most High, and I rest under the shadow of the Almighty. I am not exposed to the chaos of the world—I am hidden in Your presence. Your nearness is my shelter, and Your love is my safety.

I don't need to strive to feel secure. I am already covered. I don't need to fear the unknown. I am resting under Your wings. You are my safe place—my shield, my comfort, my quiet. In You, I find not just peace, but protection. I settle in, fully confident that I am guarded by Your hand.

I declare that no storm can shake me. No threat can reach me. I am covered, sheltered, and at peace. This evening, I abide—not as a visitor, but as a child at home in Your presence. My rest is not shallow—it is sacred.

In Jesus' name, Amen.

DAY 10

Release

Forgiveness Frees My Soul

> bearing with one another, and forgiving each other, if any man has a complaint against any; even as Christ forgave you, so you also do.
> —Colossians 3:13 WEB

Father, this evening I release every offense and every wrong committed against me. I choose to forgive—not because it was easy, not because it was deserved, but because I have been forgiven much. You call me to bear with others, to extend grace as freely as I have received it. And so, I obey—not just with my words, but with my heart. I let go of the grudge. I surrender the bitterness. I release the silent anger that tries to steal my joy.

I will not carry the poison of unforgiveness into this evening. I forgive the words that cut me, the silence that hurt me, the actions that wounded me. I release the need to be repaid or understood. My healing does not depend on their apology—it depends on Your grace. And Your grace is enough. Your mercy is my strength. I release, and I rise.

I declare that I am free from the bondage of bitterness. I am not held hostage by what others did. I am healed because I have chosen the higher road. I forgive, I bless, and I move forward. My evening is light. My heart is free. My soul is clear. Forgiveness is my freedom song.

In Jesus' name, Amen.

Renew

Victory Breathes New Strength

> But thanks be to God, who gives us the victory through our Lord Jesus Christ. Therefore, my beloved brothers, be steadfast, immovable, always abounding in the Lord's work, because you know that your labor is not in vain in the Lord.
> —1 Corinthians 15:57-58 WEB

Lord, I thank You this evening for the victory that is already mine through Jesus Christ. I may have fought some battles today—spiritually, emotionally, even mentally—but I'm not defeated. I am standing, because You've given me the strength to endure. I don't press on in my own might; I press on in the power of the One who already overcame.

I ask for a renewal of purpose and passion this evening. Let weariness melt away, and let the joy of victory rise up in me. Let the truth that my labor in You is never in vain energize me again. Even if I didn't see all the results I hoped for today, I will not be moved. My efforts are not wasted. My obedience matters. My fight is not in vain.

I declare that I am steadfast and immovable, always abounding in the work of the Lord. Victory isn't just my future—it's my present mindset. I am renewed with fresh confidence, fresh fire, and fresh faith. I will not give up. I will not back down. I am victorious, and I live like it.

In Jesus' name, Amen.

Refocus

Taking Every Thought Captive

> throwing down imaginations and every high thing that is exalted against the knowledge of God, and bringing every thought into captivity to the obedience of Christ;
> —2 Corinthians 10:5 WEB

Father, this evening I bring my mind before You. I know the battles of the day have not just been around me—they've been within me. Thoughts that questioned, doubted, or criticized tried to take root. But tonight, I take every thought captive to obey Christ. I refuse to let rogue thoughts dictate my emotions or decisions. I bring them into submission under the truth of Your Word.

I refocus my mind on what is pure, noble, and true. I will not allow thoughts of fear, comparison, defeat, or insecurity to rule me. They must bow to the Lordship of Christ. I put on the mind of Christ tonight. I choose clarity over confusion, truth over lies, and faith over fear. Let Your Word cleanse my inner world. Let Your truth stabilize me again.

I declare that my mind is guarded and governed by truth. I will not be ruled by feelings or falsehoods. I walk in mental freedom. My thoughts are aligned with heaven. Peace reigns in my soul, and clarity is my companion. I refocus with purpose, and I rest in truth. In Jesus' name, Amen.

REBUILD

CALLED BACK TO PURPOSE

> They will walk after Yahweh, who will roar like a lion; for he will roar, and the children will come trembling from the west. They will come trembling like a bird out of Egypt, and like a dove out of the land of Assyria; and I will settle them in their houses," says Yahweh.
> —Hosea 11:10-11 WEB

Lord, this evening I thank You that even when life pulls me off course, Your Spirit calls me back. Just as You drew Israel like a lion to return to their dwelling, You are calling me back to purpose, passion, and identity. Even if I've drifted, You are restoring the roar within me. You are rebuilding the parts of me that became scattered in the noise and pressure of life.

I respond to Your call with a willing heart. Rebuild the broken walls of my confidence. Reconstruct the foundations of my obedience. Restore the joy of walking in my divine assignment. I'm not too far gone. I'm not too broken. You are the God who rebuilds from ashes and resurrects purpose from the dust. I open my heart again to be reestablished.

I declare that I am returning to strength. I am returning to the fullness of who You've called me to be. My identity is secure. My voice is rising. My purpose is being reignited. I'm not lost—I'm being rebuilt. I hear You calling, and I am coming home to destiny. In Jesus' name, Amen.

Rest

Safe Sleep, Secure Heart

> When you lie down, you will not be afraid. Yes, you will lie down, and your sleep will be sweet.
> —Proverbs 3:24 WEB

Father, I end this day in the peace that only You can give. You promised that when I lie down, I will not be afraid, and that my sleep will be sweet. So I cast away every lingering tension, every creeping worry, and every concern that tried to follow me into the evening. I am safe under Your care. I am secure in Your presence.

Even before my body finds sleep, my spirit enters rest. I choose not to replay the day in frustration or anxiety. I choose to release the need for control and embrace the rhythm of grace. You are watching over me. You are covering me with love. I have no need to fear the dark or dread the unknown. Your presence is my pillow, and Your promises are my peace.

I declare that I will sleep in safety and rise in strength. My rest is not random—it is divine. My thoughts are calm. My soul is still. Peace surrounds me like a shield, and grace carries me into the night. I rest without fear, because I rest in You.

In Jesus' name, Amen.

DAY 11

RELEASE

MERCY HAS THE FINAL SAY

> Who is a God like you, who pardons iniquity, and passes over the disobedience of the remnant of his heritage? He doesn't retain his anger forever, because he delights in loving kindness. He will again have compassion on us. He will tread our iniquities under foot; and you will cast all their sins into the depths of the sea.
> —Micah 7:18-19 WEB

Father, this evening I thank You for being a God who does not stay angry forever but delights in showing mercy. I bring before You every weight of guilt, every burden of shame, and every memory that tries to condemn me. I release it all at Your feet. I surrender the lingering effects of my past, and I trust in the power of Your mercy to wash me clean and carry me forward.

You do not hold my sins against me. You have cast them into the depths of the sea, never to be retrieved. So why should I carry what You've already buried? I refuse to let condemnation rob me of peace. I release the accusations of the enemy and the lies I've told myself. I let mercy rewrite the narrative of my evening.

I declare that mercy has the final word over my life. I am not my worst moment. I am not my past failure. I am redeemed, restored, and released by grace. I walk into this evening covered in compassion and clothed in forgiveness. I am light, because the burden is gone.

In Jesus' name, Amen.

RENEW

SOARING AGAIN WITH NEW STRENGTH

> [Praise Yahweh], who satisfies your desire with good things, so that your youth is renewed like the eagle's.
> —Psalms 103:5 WEB

Lord, as this evening settles in, I turn to You for renewal. You satisfy my desires with good things, so that my youth is renewed like the eagle's. Where this day has left me depleted—physically, emotionally, or spiritually—I lean into Your goodness and draw strength from Your abundance. You are not a God who leaves me drained; You are the God who restores my vitality.

Breathe life back into tired bones. Reignite my passion for what matters. Fill the empty places with joy, the weary places with wonder, and the dull places with divine spark. I am not too far gone. I'm not past restoration. Your goodness is reviving me, even now.

I declare that my strength is being renewed. My hope is being lifted. My joy is being restored. I will not end this day in exhaustion—I will end it with fresh wind in my spirit. I am being made new from the inside out, and I receive it. In Jesus' name, Amen.

REFOCUS

TEACH ME TO SEE AGAIN

> Show me your ways, Yahweh. Teach me your paths. Guide me in your truth, and teach me, For you are the God of my salvation, I wait for you all day long.
> —Psalms 25:4-5 WEB

Father, this evening I ask You to show me Your ways. The noise of the day may have blurred my vision, but now I sit in stillness and ask You to teach me, lead me, and guide me in Your truth. You are my God and my Savior, and I wait on You—not for answers only, but for alignment.

Help me refocus not just on what I'm doing, but on why I'm doing it. Redirect the intentions of my heart. Illuminate the path You've laid out, and help me discern the difference between distraction and direction. I fix my eyes on Your presence and tune my ears to Your voice.

I declare that I am being guided by the Spirit of truth. I will not wander in confusion or be ruled by uncertainty. You are showing me the way, one step at a time. My heart is aligned. My mind is clear. My focus is restored.

In Jesus' name, Amen.

REBUILD

PRISONER OF HOPE NO MORE

> Turn to the stronghold, you prisoners of hope! Even today
> I declare that I will restore double to you.
> —Zechariah 9:12 WEB

Lord, this evening I return to the stronghold—not as a captive of fear, but as a prisoner of hope. I've seen discouragement, delay, and even defeat—but I refuse to stay there. I hear You saying, "I will restore to you double." And I believe it. You are rebuilding my hope, not just to survive, but to flourish again.

Hope is not fragile—it is fierce. And I choose to cling to it tonight. You are reviving my faith to believe for the impossible. You are restoring joy where grief once sat. You are mending dreams that I thought were too broken to breathe again. I'm not going back—I'm coming back stronger.

I declare that restoration is in motion. I'm not hopeless—I am hope-filled. I'm not stuck—I'm being rebuilt. The prison of disappointment is breaking, and a fortress of hope is rising in its place. I am a prisoner of hope, and restoration is my reward.

In Jesus' name, Amen.

Rest

I Wait in Quiet Confidence

> For the Chief Musician. To Jeduthun. A Psalm by David.
> My soul rests in God alone. My salvation is from him. He alone is my rock and my salvation, my fortress— I will never be greatly shaken.
> —Psalms 62:1-2 WEB

Father, this evening I step away from striving and into stillness. I wait quietly for You alone, because my hope comes from You. You are my rock and my salvation, my fortress—I will not be shaken. In the chaos of life, You are the calm I run to. In the noise of the world, You are the quiet that restores me.

I don't need to rush. I don't need to fix everything. I don't even need to understand everything. I just need to be still and know that You are God. Your presence anchors me. Your strength sustains me. Your peace surrounds me.

I declare that my rest is not found in circumstance but in Christ. I will not be tossed by fear or overwhelmed by pressure. I will lie down in peace. I will rise in strength. In You, I am safe. In You, I am settled. I wait, and in the waiting—I rest.

In Jesus' name, Amen.

DAY 12

RELEASE

BURDENS LIFTED, BLESSINGS RECEIVED

> Blessed be the Lord, who daily bears our burdens, even the God who is our salvation. Selah. God is to us a God of deliverance. To Yahweh, the Lord, belongs escape from death.
> —Psalms 68:19-20 WEB

Father, this evening I lift up every weight I've carried throughout the day—every emotional load, mental pressure, and spiritual heaviness—and I lay it at Your feet. You daily bear my burdens, and tonight I take You at Your Word. I release the stress of trying to do it all, the fear of not being enough, and the silent fatigue that builds up in my soul. I wasn't made to carry what You've already offered to take.

You are not only my Deliverer; You are the One who loads me with benefits. So I release the burden and open my hands to receive the blessing. I release striving and receive strength. I release tension and receive peace. I release the pressure to perform and receive the joy of simply being Yours.

I declare that this evening is a divine exchange. My burdens are leaving and Your blessings are landing. I will not carry anxiety into the night. I am free, I am light, and I am cared for. You are my burden-bearer and my soul's refreshment. In Jesus' name, Amen.

RENEW

YOU SATISFY MY SOUL AGAIN

> For I have satiated the weary soul, and I have replenished every sorrowful soul."
> —Jeremiah 31:25 WEB

Lord, this evening I come to You, weary in body and soul, but with a heart ready for refreshing. Your Word says You satisfy the weary and replenish the faint. So I stand under the fountain of Your faithfulness and let Your presence restore what the day has drained from me. You don't just refill me; You renew me.

Where I've poured out—through decisions, conversations, or silent endurance—I ask for divine replenishment. Let laughter return where sorrow sat. Let clarity come where confusion lingered. Let a fresh wind of joy blow away the residue of fatigue. I want to feel Your nearness as real as breath, as close as the rhythm of my heart.

I declare that I am being satisfied and replenished. I am not forgotten. I am not overlooked. The same God who saw my effort sees my emptiness—and is filling me again. I rest in renewal. I breathe in grace. I rise in quiet strength.

In Jesus' name, Amen.

REFOCUS

WISDOM FOR THE WAY FORWARD

> But if any of you lacks wisdom, let him ask of God, who gives to all liberally and without reproach; and it will be given to him.
> —James 1:5 WEB

Father, this evening I turn from the voices that clutter my thinking and seek the clarity that comes only from You. Your Word promises that when I lack wisdom, I can ask—and You will give generously. So I ask now, not just for answers, but for understanding. Not just direction, but discernment. Lead me in the way I should go.

I quiet the noise of my own assumptions and opinions, and I yield to Your voice. Teach me to see beyond the obvious. Help me to pause before reacting, to wait before deciding, to listen before speaking. Wisdom is not just about knowing what to do, but about doing it with Your timing, Your tone, and Your truth.

I declare that my mind is sharp, my spirit is discerning, and my focus is fixed on You. I will not be pulled in every direction. I will not move ahead in confusion. I walk in wisdom, because You are faithful to give it. I refocus now—not on problems, but on Your perfect counsel.

In Jesus' name, Amen.

Rebuild

Joy Rising from the Ruins

> Those who sow in tears will reap in joy. He who goes out weeping, carrying seed for sowing, will certainly come again with joy, carrying his sheaves.
> —Psalms 126:5-6 WEB

Lord, I thank You this evening that You are turning my tears into testimonies. You see the seeds I've sown in sorrow, and You promise that joy will be the harvest. I may have cried through decisions, worshipped through pain, and labored through trials—but not one tear has been wasted. You are the God of restoration, and You are rebuilding joy in me tonight.

Even when the ground felt barren, I kept walking. Even when the promise seemed far, I kept believing. And now, I sense the shift. I feel the breakthrough. Joy is rising from the ruins. Hope is blooming where sorrow had been. You are faithful to bring in the sheaves with rejoicing.

I declare that this is not the end—it's the beginning of the rebuild. I am moving from sorrow to singing, from mourning to dancing, from weeping to witnessing. My harvest is coming, and joy is already here. You are rebuilding my spirit from the inside out.

In Jesus' name, Amen.

REST

RESTING IN GRACE-FILLED SPACES

> Yahweh says, "The people who survive the sword found favor in the wilderness; even Israel, when I went to cause him to rest."
> —Jeremiah 31:2 WEB

Father, this evening I rest in the assurance that You give grace in the wilderness. Even when life has felt dry or uncertain, You've been with me. You've led me gently, spoken kindly, and sustained me in every season. You never left me wandering alone. You found me and gave me rest where I least expected it.

I settle into the space You've carved out for me tonight—not just a physical place, but a heart-place where grace flows freely. I don't have to fight for rest; I just have to receive it. I don't have to earn peace; I just have to trust. The wilderness didn't destroy me—it made me ready for stillness.

I declare that I am resting in grace. The journey has not been easy, but it has brought me to this moment of divine peace. I breathe deep. I release worry. I rest—not because the way ahead is clear, but because the One who leads me is near. My soul is safe. My evening is blessed.

In Jesus' name, Amen.

DAY 13

RELEASE

LETTING GO TO TRUST AGAIN

> Trust in Yahweh with all your heart, and don't lean on your own understanding. In all your ways acknowledge him, and he will make your paths straight.
> —Proverbs 3:5-6 WEB

Father, this evening I surrender the need to understand everything. I release the tight grip of control and the fear that comes with uncertainty. I've tried to figure out the "why," the "when," and the "how," but tonight I choose to trust You with all my heart. I lean not on my own understanding, because my wisdom is limited—but Yours is perfect.

I lay at Your feet every anxious thought and every question I can't answer. I release the weight of trying to make things happen in my strength. You are the One who directs my paths, and I believe You're working behind the scenes even when I can't see it. Trust is my worship tonight. Let every part of me align with that truth.

I declare that I am not ruled by fear or confusion. I am anchored in trust. I release the burden of control, and I embrace the peace that comes from believing in Your plan. My steps are ordered. My heart is secure. I let go—and I trust again. In Jesus' name, Amen.

Renew

Guided and Watered Again

> And Yahweh will guide you continually, and satisfy your soul in dry places, and make your bones strong; and you shall be like a watered garden, and like a spring of water, whose waters don't fail.
> —Isaiah 58:11 WEB

Lord, this evening I thank You for being my Guide. When the day has been long and my soul has been dry, You lead me with tenderness and sustain me with Your goodness. You make me like a well-watered garden—fruitful, alive, and full of hope. I may have felt drained, but You are the Source that never runs dry.

Refresh me, Father. Where my spirit has grown tired, let fresh waters flow. Where my strength has been depleted, let divine vitality rise up again. You are not only guiding me—you are feeding me along the way. Your presence is nourishment, and Your peace is my renewal.

I declare that I am flourishing, even in dry seasons. I am renewed in the deepest parts of my soul. I am not abandoned; I am watered. I am not lost; I am led. You are restoring me right now, and I receive Your life-giving touch.

In Jesus' name, Amen.

REFOCUS

CHOOSING WHAT REALLY MATTERS

> Jesus answered her, "Martha, Martha, you are anxious and troubled about many things, but one thing is needed. Mary has chosen the good part, which will not be taken away from her."
> —Luke 10:41-42 WEB

Jesus, this evening I quiet my heart and choose what matters most—time with You. Like Martha, I've been busy with many things. But like Mary, I want to sit at Your feet and listen. I let go of the mental noise, the schedule, and the never-ending list of responsibilities. You said one thing is necessary—and I choose it now.

I refocus my evening on the beauty of Your presence. Not on the chaos of the day, not on the pressure of performance, but on the simplicity of being with You. Let my heart realign with Your voice. Let my mind be stilled by Your nearness. Let me find joy not in what I do, but in who You are.

I declare that I am focused again. I'm not scattered—I'm centered. I'm not striving—I'm sitting. You are my portion, and I lack nothing when I'm with You. This is where my soul finds rest—in choosing You above all.

In Jesus' name, Amen.

Rebuild

Healing in the Rising Light

> But to you who fear my name shall the sun of righteousness arise with healing in its wings. You will go out, and leap like calves of the stall.
> —Malachi 4:2 WEB

Lord, I thank You this evening that You are rising over me like the sun of righteousness, with healing in Your wings. I've endured the dark places—pain that lingered, sorrow that ran deep—but now I sense the dawn. You are rebuilding my soul through healing. Every place that was cracked by life is being touched by Your light.

I don't need to understand every wound to receive healing. I only need to look to You. Let Your light penetrate the hidden places—the emotions I've buried, the memories I've avoided. Let joy return where sadness settled. Let hope rise where despair tried to root itself. Your healing is restoring me completely.

I declare that I am rising in joy and running in freedom. The light has come, and it is chasing away every shadow. I am healed in my heart, in my mind, and in my identity. You are rebuilding me with gentle strength and radiant grace.

In Jesus' name, Amen.

Rest

The Breaker of Bondage

> It will happen in the day that Yahweh will give you rest from your sorrow, from your trouble, and from the hard service in which you were made to serve,
> —Isaiah 14:3 WEB

Father, this evening I rest in the promise that You give me relief from suffering, turmoil, and bondage. The pressures of life may have pressed hard today, but they will not define my night. You are the One who breaks oppression. You silence the tormentor. You give Your people rest—not just physical, but emotional and spiritual rest from the battles that rage within.

I step away from internal warfare. I let go of the mental weight and emotional labor. I find stillness in Your victory. You have broken the yoke. You have lifted the burden. I rest tonight as one who has been set free—not just from sin, but from stress, sorrow, and striving.

I declare that I am resting under divine relief. Bondages are broken. Struggles are silenced. Peace surrounds me like a shield. I lie down with joy. I rise with strength. I sleep in freedom, because You have given me rest from the battle.

In Jesus' name, Amen.

DAY 14

RELEASE

I LAY DOWN WEAKNESS

> He gives power to the weak. He increases the strength of him who has no might.
> —Isaiah 40:29 WEB

Father, this evening I come to You, not pretending to be strong but bringing my weakness honestly. You give power to the faint and strength to those with no might. I release the pressure to pretend, the exhaustion I've pushed through, and the hidden struggles I've tried to carry alone. I lay down my weariness and receive Your strength.

I release every internal battle—mental fatigue, emotional heaviness, spiritual discouragement—and I exchange them for Your supernatural power. I don't have to have it all together. You delight in lifting those who wait on You. So I stretch my soul before You, knowing You will meet me in the place of my need.

I declare that weakness is not my identity—it is the platform for Your strength. I let go of self-reliance and embrace divine support. I am being renewed. I am being lifted. My evening is not ending in defeat, but in dependence on the One who never grows weary.

In Jesus' name, Amen.

Renew

Revived and Raised Again

> "Come! Let's return to Yahweh; for he has torn us to pieces, and he will heal us; he has injured us, and he will bind up our wounds. After two days he will revive us. On the third day he will raise us up, and we will live before him.
> —Hosea 6:1-2 WEB

Lord, this evening I come to the Healer of hearts and the Restorer of life. You are the One who revives what seems dead, who breathes life where hope has faded. I return to You with open wounds and weary places, trusting that You will bind me up and raise me again. After every fall, You restore. After every wound, You heal.

Where I've been broken, let Your restoration begin. Where I've walked through dryness, let refreshing rain fall again. You don't just repair—you revive. Let resurrection power touch every area of my life that's grown cold, distant, or numb. Raise my joy. Raise my passion. Raise my strength to believe again.

I declare that revival is happening in me. I'm not stuck in a season of despair—I'm stepping into renewal. I'm being lifted up by Your grace and restored in every way. I rise because You raise me. I live because You've touched me.

In Jesus' name, Amen.

Refocus

Delight in His Direction

> Also delight yourself in Yahweh, and he will give you the desires of your heart. Commit your way to Yahweh. Trust also in him, and he will do this:
> —Psalms 37:4-5 WEB

Father, this evening I choose to quiet my striving and fix my focus on You. You have not called me to chase after the world's rewards, but to delight in You—and from that place, You promise to shape my desires and direct my steps. So I surrender every ambition, every longing, and every plan to You.

Teach me to delight in You again—not in accomplishments, approval, or outcomes, but in simply knowing You. Let my heart rest in Your presence, and from that place, realign my purpose. As I commit my way to You, I trust You to act. You are not silent or distant. You are guiding me, even now.

I declare that my heart is being purified and my path is being clarified. I do not walk blindly—I walk in trust. My focus is not scattered—it is steady on You. I delight in You, and You are aligning my life to reflect Your will.

In Jesus' name, Amen.

Rebuild

You Have Not Abandoned Me

> For we are bondservants; yet our God has not forsaken us in our bondage, but has extended loving kindness to us in the sight of the kings of Persia, to revive us, to set up the house of our God, and to repair its ruins, and to give us a wall in Judah and in Jerusalem.
> —Ezra 9:9 WEB

Lord, this evening I praise You for being the God who revives, restores, and rebuilds. Though I have known captivity—seasons of brokenness, regret, or spiritual dryness—you have not left me in ruins. You have extended mercy, lifted my head, and given me new life. You have revived me to rebuild what I thought was lost forever.

You are reestablishing my foundation, brick by brick, truth by truth. You are planting hope where shame once lived. You are restoring my purpose and rebuilding trust in places that were shaken. My life is not a pile of rubble—it is a temple under construction by Your hands. You are the Master Builder, and You are not finished with me.

I declare that this is not the end—it is a rebuilding season. I am walking out of ruin into restoration. I am rising, not in my own strength, but in Your mercy and faithfulness. You have revived me for this very moment, and I step into it with gratitude.

In Jesus' name, Amen.

Rest

Silent Trust, Steady Peace

> Rest in Yahweh, and wait patiently for him. Don't fret because of him who prospers in his way, because of the man who makes wicked plots happen.
> —Psalms 37:7 WEB

Father, this evening I choose stillness over striving. I rest not just in body, but in soul. I quiet my heart before You and wait patiently, trusting in Your perfect timing. I release every impulse to rush ahead or fix things myself. You are working, even in the waiting. You are faithful, even in the silence.

I will not let worry steal my peace or impatience rob my joy. I rest in the assurance that You see, You know, and You care. My trust is not in what I see, but in who You are. I may not have all the answers, but I have the Anchor—and that is enough.

I declare that my soul is at rest. I am not shaken by delays or setbacks. I am confident in Your goodness and steadfast in Your promises. I wait in peace. I rest in faith. I lie down in security, knowing that You hold all things together.

In Jesus' name, Amen.

DAY 15

RELEASE

HE HEARS AND DELIVERS

> The righteous cry, and Yahweh hears, and delivers them out of all their troubles.
> —Psalms 34:17 WEB

Father, this evening I release every cry, every groan, and every silent prayer I've held within. You have heard the cry of the righteous, and You promise deliverance—not from some, but from all of our troubles. So I let go of the burden to fix everything myself. I surrender the pressure to be strong, the need to pretend I'm fine, and the fear that my pain has gone unnoticed.

You see me, and You respond with power. Even when the answers are not immediate, I trust that You are working deliverance in ways I cannot yet see. I release the ache that has clung to my heart, and I receive the comfort of Your presence. I trust that You are not only listening, but You are moving on my behalf.

I declare that my prayers have not gone unheard. My tears are not wasted. The Lord has heard, and He will answer. I release discouragement, and I receive divine intervention. I release fear, and I embrace faith. My evening is covered with the assurance that I am not alone and not forsaken. In Jesus' name, Amen.

RENEW

ANCHORED IN UNSHAKABLE HOPE

> This hope we have as an anchor of the soul, a hope both sure and steadfast and entering into that which is within the veil;
> —Hebrews 6:19 WEB

Lord, this evening I thank You for the anchor of hope. In the shifting tides of life, in the storms that rage within and around me, Your hope holds me steady. I may have felt tossed today—by bad news, heavy conversations, or uncertain decisions—but I anchor my soul once again in Your unchanging Word.

You are faithful, and Your promises are sure. Though I may not see the outcome yet, I will not let go of the rope of hope. Let Your Spirit renew me tonight with strength that surpasses weariness, with confidence that overcomes delay, and with joy that breaks through the fog. Hope is not a feeling—it's my foundation.

I declare that I am rooted, grounded, and held firm. I will not drift. I will not sink. I am anchored in Christ, and my hope will not disappoint. I rise this evening in renewal, carrying a heart full of trust and a mind fixed on Your faithfulness.

In Jesus' name, Amen.

REFOCUS

My Labor Is Not in Vain

> Let's not be weary in doing good, for we will reap in due season, if we don't give up.
> —Galatians 6:9 WEB

Father, this evening I refocus my heart and realign my perspective. I've labored, I've prayed, I've persevered—and some days, it feels like the harvest is still far off. But Your Word reminds me not to grow weary in well-doing. So tonight, I choose to silence the lie that says, "It's not working." I choose to believe that in due season, I will reap if I do not give up.

Help me to see my efforts through heaven's eyes. Remind me that obedience matters, that faithfulness bears fruit, and that nothing done in love is wasted. Reignite my joy in the journey. Let me not be so consumed with results that I forget to rejoice in the process. Refocus me on Your timing, not mine.

I declare that my hands are blessed. My labor is sacred. My faithfulness is not forgotten. I am not working in vain—I am sowing in the Spirit, and a harvest is coming. I fix my eyes again on You, and I keep going with renewed strength.

In Jesus' name, Amen.

Rebuild

From Rubble to Precious Stones

> "You afflicted, tossed with storms, and not comforted, behold, I will set your stones in beautiful colors, and lay your foundations with sapphires. I will make your pinnacles of rubies, your gates of sparkling jewels, and all your walls of precious stones.
> —Isaiah 54:11-12 WEB

Lord, I thank You this evening that You are the Master Builder. Though life has shaken my foundation and storms have scattered my peace, You are rebuilding me with precious stones. You are taking what once looked like ruins and turning it into beauty. You are laying firm foundations of peace, righteousness, and joy.

You've seen every place where my heart was battered—by rejection, failure, or loss. But You don't discard the broken pieces. You refashion them into strength. You are not just patching things up—you are creating something more glorious than before. I give You permission to rebuild me Your way.

I declare that I am being rebuilt with divine craftsmanship. My life is being formed with heavenly material. Where there was instability, there will now be strength. Where there was sorrow, there will now be splendor. The Lord is rebuilding me—and this structure will not be shaken.

In Jesus' name, Amen.

Rest

Peace Be with Me

> As they said these things, Jesus himself stood among them, and said to them, "Peace be to you."
> —Luke 24:36 WEB

Jesus, this evening I receive Your peace. Just as You stood in the midst of fearful disciples and declared, "Peace be with you," I receive that same Word into my atmosphere, my thoughts, and my emotions. Let Your peace settle into every unsettled place. Let it silence every voice of anxiety, every echo of stress, every noise of unrest.

You are not a distant Savior. You are present in the middle of my room, my day, my thoughts—and You bring peace that the world cannot offer. I release the tension from today, and I open my heart to Your stillness. Not because everything is fixed, but because You are here. That is enough.

I declare that peace reigns over this evening. I am not agitated, I am not anxious—I am aligned with the Prince of Peace. I welcome Your calming presence and lay down every burden. My rest is holy. My rest is whole.

In Jesus' name, Amen.

DAY 16

RELEASE

FREE FROM GUILT AND SHAME

> There is therefore now no condemnation to those who are in Christ Jesus, who don't walk according to the flesh, but according to the Spirit. For the law of the Spirit of life in Christ Jesus made me free from the law of sin and of death.
> —Romans 8:1-2 WEB

Father, this evening I boldly release every trace of guilt, shame, and condemnation. Your Word declares there is now no condemnation for those who are in Christ Jesus—for I have been set free from the law of sin and death. I refuse to carry the weight of what You have already forgiven. I lay down the mental torment, the self-accusation, and the quiet regrets that try to chain me to my past.

I walk in the freedom You purchased with Your blood. I am not defined by my yesterday—I am defined by Your grace. I release the need to replay failures in my mind. I release the weight of people's expectations and opinions. I stand on the truth that I am forgiven, free, and deeply loved.

I declare that I am no longer a prisoner to shame. I am walking in the liberty of the Spirit. I am not under condemnation—I am under covenant. My soul is unburdened, and my evening is full of peace. I release, and I rise in freedom. In Jesus' name, Amen.

Renew

God's Not Finished With Me

> being confident of this very thing, that he who began a good work in you will complete it until the day of Jesus Christ.
> —Philippians 1:6 WEB

Lord, this evening I rest in the truth that You, who began a good work in me, will carry it on to completion. I release the pressure to have it all figured out. I surrender the discouragement of unfinished progress and unmet goals. You are not done with me, and that gives me hope. You don't leave things halfway. You are a faithful finisher.

Where I've grown tired of waiting or weary in the process, breathe fresh life into me. Remind me that I am not behind—I'm on Your timetable. You are shaping me, stretching me, and growing me with every step. I don't need to see the full picture—I just need to trust the One holding the brush.

I declare that I am under construction by divine hands. I am being renewed daily, formed for Your glory, and prepared for every good work. I welcome the work You're doing in me, knowing that the end result will reflect Your goodness. I'm not stuck—I'm becoming.

In Jesus' name, Amen.

REFOCUS

FIX MY HOPE FULLY

> Therefore prepare your minds for action, be sober, and set your hope fully on the grace that will be brought to you at the revelation of Jesus Christ—
> —1 Peter 1:13 WEB

Father, this evening I gather the scattered pieces of my attention and fix my hope fully on You. I prepare my mind for action. I set my heart on grace. I silence distractions, realign my focus, and renew my perspective. My hope is not in the news, in people, or in my own strength. My hope is in the living Christ, who reigns now and forever.

This evening, I refuse to let fear dominate my thoughts or anxiety cloud my vision. I choose to think with eternity in mind and live with purpose in my spirit. Let every idle thought be replaced with intention. Let every wandering fear be arrested by Your Word.

I declare that I have a focused mind and a hopeful heart. I am not driven by circumstances—I am anchored in grace. I set my eyes on what is unseen and eternal. I live in clarity, not confusion. My hope is secure.

In Jesus' name, Amen.

Rebuild

Healing the Land Within

> if my people, who are called by my name, will humble themselves, pray, seek my face, and turn from their wicked ways; then I will hear from heaven, will forgive their sin, and will heal their land.
> —2 Chronicles 7:14 WEB

Lord, this evening I humble myself before You. I turn my heart fully toward You and seek Your face—not just for breakthrough, but for cleansing and alignment. You promise that when Your people humble themselves, pray, seek You, and turn from their wicked ways, You will hear, forgive, and heal. I bring not only my life, but my land—the places in my soul that need restoration.

Heal the dry ground of discouragement. Restore the broken walls of faith. Rebuild the foundation of obedience. Where my love has grown cold, rekindle the fire. Where my spiritual vision has dimmed, let fresh clarity come. You are not just repairing me, You are restoring righteousness in me.

I declare that healing is flowing into every part of my being. You are rebuilding my inner life—stronger, purer, and more surrendered than before. You are healing my land, and I will walk in the fruit of restoration.

In Jesus' name, Amen.

Rest

My Heart Is at Peace

> Peace I leave with you. My peace I give to you; not as the world gives, give I to you. Don't let your heart be troubled, neither let it be fearful.
> —John 14:27 WEB

Jesus, this evening I receive the peace that only You can give. Not the fragile, fleeting kind the world offers, but the kind that calms storms and silences fear. Let that peace now rule my heart and steady my soul. I surrender the turmoil, the overthinking, and the restless energy that's tried to follow me into the evening.

You are near, and where You are, peace reigns. I rest in the assurance that I am not alone, not forgotten, not unprotected. You are guarding my heart and mind with peace that surpasses understanding. Let that peace settle over every thought and undergird every emotion.

I declare that my atmosphere is filled with divine stillness. My spirit is calm. My heart is quiet. I rest—not in escape, but in presence. I will not be shaken, because the Prince of Peace is with me.

In Jesus' name, Amen.

DAY 17

RELEASE

I AM FREE INDEED

> If therefore the Son makes you free, you will be free indeed.
> —John 8:36 WEB

Father, this evening I release every lie, every bondage, and every limitation that has kept me from walking in the full freedom You've already given me. Your Son has set me free—not conditionally, not temporarily—but truly and completely. I will no longer allow guilt, fear, or shame to bind me. I shake off the chains of the past, the opinions of others, and the false identities I've carried for too long.

You didn't free me to live afraid. You didn't deliver me so I could stay bound in my mind or emotions. I am free to walk in righteousness, to love without fear, to live without apology. I declare that I am no longer held hostage by what used to hold me down. Freedom is my inheritance—and I receive it fully tonight.

I stand tall in the liberty of Christ. I will no longer return to old cycles. I will not shrink back into old mindsets. I am free indeed—liberated in heart, loosed in spirit, and alive in truth.

In Jesus' name, Amen.

Renew

He's Making All Things New

> He who sits on the throne said, "Behold, I am making all things new." He said, "Write, for these words of God are faithful and true."
> —Revelation 21:5 WEB

Lord, this evening I open my heart to the wonder of Your restoration. You are the God who makes all things new—not just some things, not just outward things, but every part of my life. Where things have felt old, tired, broken, or beyond repair—You step in with resurrection power and speak renewal. Nothing is too far gone for You.

Breathe freshness into my soul. Wash away the residue of disappointment. Remove the sting of the past and replace it with the fragrance of new beginnings. Let this evening mark a shift—from decay to renewal, from weary to vibrant, from bitter to blessed. I declare that newness is not just coming—it's already begun.

I receive Your renewing touch in my mind, my purpose, and my relationships. I declare that restoration is in motion. I don't have to settle for brokenness—You are making all things new, and I welcome the change.

In Jesus' name, Amen.

REFOCUS

EYES ENLIGHTENED WITH HOPE

> having the eyes of your hearts enlightened, that you may know what is the hope of his calling, and what are the riches of the glory of his inheritance in the saints,
> —Ephesians 1:18 WEB

Father, this evening I ask You to enlighten the eyes of my heart. I've seen too much with natural vision—now I need to see from a heavenly view. Give me clarity, Lord—not just to make decisions, but to see purpose. Let the fog lift. Let the distractions fall away. Help me to lock eyes with destiny again.

You've called me to a hope that does not disappoint. So I silence every lie that tells me I'm too late, too broken, or too far behind. I fix my gaze on what You've promised—not on what I've lost. I refocus on the riches of Your inheritance and the power that's already working within me.

I declare that I am no longer wandering blindly—I'm walking with focused vision. My eyes are enlightened, my heart is steady, and my direction is clear. I see again—and what I see is hope.

In Jesus' name, Amen.

Rebuild

The Lord Roars Over Me

> Yahweh will roar from Zion, and thunder from Jerusalem; and the heavens and the earth will shake; but Yahweh will be a refuge to his people, and a stronghold to the children of Israel. "So you will know that I am Yahweh, your God, dwelling in Zion, my holy mountain. Then Jerusalem will be holy, and no strangers will pass through her any more.
> —Joel 3:16-17 WEB

Lord, this evening I take comfort in the sound of Your roar. You are not silent when Your children are under pressure. You thunder from Zion and shake the heavens in defense of Your people. You are roaring over every area where the enemy tried to destroy, and You are establishing my security in You once again.

I may have been shaken, but I was never abandoned. I may have been wounded, but I was never disqualified. You are restoring my identity as holy, set apart, and fortified by Your Spirit. You are rebuilding the ruins of my faith, reaffirming my calling, and reestablishing my authority as Your own.

I declare that I dwell in safety because the Lord fights for me. I will not be shaken by opposition or discouraged by delays. I am a restored place—holy, strong, and secured by divine promise.

In Jesus' name, Amen.

Rest

Rest from the Labor, Not the Purpose

> I heard a voice from heaven saying, "Write, 'Blessed are the dead who die in the Lord from now on.'" "Yes," says the Spirit, "that they may rest from their labors; for their works follow with them."
> —Revelation 14:13 WEB

Father, this evening I rest—not as one who is quitting, but as one who is complete in You. Your Word says, "Blessed are those who die in the Lord… for their deeds follow them." And while I am still here, I take hold of that eternal truth: the work I do in You is never in vain. I don't labor for rest—I work from it.

I lay down the exhaustion of performance. I release the pressure to prove. I rest in the reality that my purpose continues, but my strength is drawn from grace. Let me rest well this evening, not just physically, but in soul—knowing that You are keeping account of every faithful step I take.

I declare that I am resting in legacy. My efforts are not wasted. My labor is not forgotten. You are storing up eternal fruit, and I am at peace with the pace You've set. I rest in the rhythm of heaven—unrushed, unworried, unshaken.

In Jesus' name, Amen.

DAY 18

RELEASE

BRING MY SOUL OUT

> Listen to my cry, for I am in desperate need. deliver me from my persecutors, For they are stronger than me. Bring my soul out of prison, that I may give thanks to your name. The righteous will surround me, for you will be good to me.
> —Psalms 142:6-7 WEB

Father, this evening I cry out to You from the hidden places of my soul. Hear my plea, for I am in need of deliverance. I release every prison I've built around myself—every emotional cage, mental wall, and spiritual restraint. The weight of isolation, fear, and inner torment cannot go with me into this next moment of grace. I need You to bring my soul out of captivity.

You are my portion, my strength, and my freedom. I surrender the bitterness that chained me, the wounds I didn't know how to heal, and the silence that kept me stuck. I release every false comfort and harmful coping mechanism. You are enough, and I run into Your arms, asking You to deliver me.

I declare that I am not forsaken and not forgotten. I am coming out of the prison of my past into the purpose of my future. I am not bound—I am being brought out into a spacious place, surrounded by Your goodness. This is my evening of release and restoration.

In Jesus' name, Amen.

RENEW

I HAVE POWER, LOVE, AND PEACE

> For God didn't give us a spirit of fear, but of power, love, and self-control.
> —2 Timothy 1:7 WEB

Lord, this evening I reject the spirit of fear, and I welcome the truth of who I am in You. You have not given me a spirit of fear, but of power, love, and a sound mind. I refuse to be ruled by intimidation, anxiety, or panic. I renew my heart and mind with Your strength tonight.

Let courage arise again where fear once sat. Let love cast out all tormenting thoughts. Let clarity replace confusion. Your Spirit within me is bold and peaceful at the same time—filled with strength and rooted in love. I am not powerless. I am not unstable. I am not unloved. I am renewed in identity and truth.

I declare that I carry divine authority, perfect peace, and unshakable love. Fear has no room in me. I walk boldly into my evening, covered in confidence and grounded in grace. I am mentally refreshed, emotionally restored, and spiritually secure.

In Jesus' name, Amen.

REFOCUS

SET MY HEART TO SEEK

> Now set your heart and your soul to follow Yahweh your God. Arise therefore, and build the sanctuary of Yahweh God, to bring the ark of Yahweh's covenant and the holy vessels of God into the house that is to be built for Yahweh's name."
> —1 Chronicles 22:19 WEB

Father, this evening I press pause on every other pursuit and set my heart to seek You. I refocus my attention—not on temporary tasks or passing worries, but on Your eternal presence. Like David, I prepare myself to build—first by preparing my heart. I don't just want to do for You, I want to be with You.

Let every scattered thought come into alignment. Let my motives be purified and my goals be re-centered. I refocus not just my plans, but my heart. Give me clarity in this moment to remember what truly matters: to love You, to follow You, and to hear Your voice in the stillness.

I declare that my evening is one of divine focus. I am not distracted. I am not double-minded. My eyes are on You, and my purpose is set. I seek first Your kingdom, and everything else will fall into place.

In Jesus' name, Amen.

Rebuild

Speak Life to My Dry Places

> Again he said to me, "Prophesy over these bones, and tell them, 'You dry bones, hear Yahweh's word. Thus says the Lord Yahweh to these bones: "Behold, I will cause breath to enter into you, and you will live.
> —Ezekiel 37:4-5 WEB

Lord, this evening I hear Your command: "Prophesy to these dry bones, and they shall live." So I stand in faith and speak life to every broken, brittle, and barren place within me. Where my hope has dried up, I speak resurrection. Where my purpose has withered, I declare revival. You are breathing on me again.

Rebuild what I thought was lost forever. Let the breath of Your Spirit enter my dreams, my discipline, my calling. Put flesh on the vision again. Strengthen the structure of my soul. Let divine alignment come to every disconnected piece. You are not done, and neither am I.

I declare that dry bones are rattling and rising. Restoration is in motion. Life is being rebuilt where loss once lived. I am standing again—not in my strength, but in Your Spirit.

In Jesus' name, Amen.

Rest

Be Still and Know

"Be still, and know that I am God. I will be exalted among the nations. I will be exalted in the earth."
—Psalms 46:10 WEB

Father, this evening I surrender to Your stillness. I don't have to strive, fight, or figure everything out—I just need to be still and know that You are God. In this quiet moment, I let go of every urgent thought and anxious concern. You are exalted above it all. You reign over my chaos, and You speak peace into my soul.

I choose rest—not because the problems have vanished, but because I trust the One who holds all things together. I don't need to do more to earn rest. I simply receive it as a gift from You. I lean into the gentle rhythm of Your presence and breathe deep in the silence.

I declare that I am resting in revelation. You are God, and I am Yours. I will not be moved. My heart is still. My mind is clear. My spirit is at peace. This evening, I rest in the sacred quiet of Your love. In Jesus' name, Amen.

DAY 19

RELEASE

YOU HEARD MY CRY

> I called on your name, Yahweh, out of the lowest dungeon. You heard my voice: "Don't hide your ear from my sighing, and my cry." You came near in the day that I called on you. You said, "Don't be afraid."
> —Lamentations 3:55-57 WEB

Father, this evening I release every cry that's risen from the depths of my soul. In the quiet moments when I didn't have the words—just groans, sighs, or silent weeping—You heard me. From the pit of despair, I called on Your name, and You drew near. You didn't turn away. You didn't hide. You leaned in and answered.

So I let go of the fear that says I'm unheard, unseen, or forgotten. I release the heaviness of thinking I must figure it out alone. I release the shame of past regrets and the dread of unknown tomorrows. You have come near, and that is all I need. I don't have to shout to be seen. You're already here.

I declare that my cries are not in vain. Heaven has heard, and help is already on the way. You are the God who responds, who rescues, who reassures. I release the burden—and receive the comfort. I am not abandoned. I am known. In Jesus' name, Amen.

RENEW

FRESH OIL FOR THE EVENING

> But you have exalted my horn like that of the wild ox. I am anointed with fresh oil.
> —Psalms 92:10 WEB

Lord, this evening I thank You for the promise of fresh oil. You have anointed me with new strength, new joy, and a fresh outpouring of Your Spirit. Where the day has drained me, where the battles have bruised me, where my heart has grown tired—Your oil flows to restore and renew.

Pour into me again. Saturate every dry and weary place. Let the oil of gladness replace the ashes of sorrow. Let Your anointing break the yoke of weariness and stir up divine energy within me. I refuse to run on yesterday's strength when You have fresh provision for me tonight.

I declare that I am being renewed right now. I am not empty—I am overflowing. I am not tired—I am empowered. I am anointed with fresh oil for the journey ahead, and nothing can stop what You've ignited in me.

In Jesus' name, Amen.

Refocus

I Will Not Be Shaken

> I have set Yahweh always before me. Because he is at my right hand, I shall not be moved.
> —Psalms 16:8 WEB

Father, this evening I fix my eyes on You. I set You continually before me, and because You are at my right hand, I will not be moved. My focus returns to Your presence, not the problems. To Your power, not my pressure. To Your promises, not my pain.

Let the distractions fade and the noise be silenced. Realign my mind to what matters. Steady my gaze so that my emotions no longer lead me—but Your truth does. I will not be shaken by what I see or hear. I will not be moved by the chaos around me. You are my anchor, and my heart is secure.

I declare that my focus is fixed, and my footing is firm. I stand, not in my own ability, but in unwavering faith. I will not be shaken—I will stand strong, with You before me and beside me.

In Jesus' name, Amen.

Rebuild

Glory After This

> 'The latter glory of this house will be greater than the former,' says Yahweh of Armies; 'and in this place I will give peace,' says Yahweh of Armies."
> —Haggai 2:9 WEB

Lord, this evening I give You praise that the glory of the latter house will be greater than the former. You are the God of greater, of increase, of restoration that exceeds the loss. What You are building in me now is not a return to what was—but a rise into something better, fuller, and more glorious.

Even where I've seen ruin, even where the foundation seemed broken, You are laying stones of peace and grace. You are rebuilding my hope with purpose. You are rewriting my story with glory. This is not the end—it's the unveiling of something far better than I imagined.

I declare that the glory is coming. The latter will be greater. The future will be brighter. What You are rebuilding in me will carry the fragrance of Your presence and the weight of Your favor.

In Jesus' name, Amen.

Rest

Every Promise Fulfilled

> "Blessed be Yahweh, who has given rest to his people Israel, according to all that he promised. There has not failed one word of all his good promise, which he promised by Moses his servant.
> —1 Kings 8:56 WEB

Father, this evening I rest in the assurance that not one of Your promises has failed. You have been faithful from generation to generation, and You are faithful to me now. I lay down my striving. I lay down the stress that comes from trying to make things happen. You've already spoken, and You will bring it to pass.

Let my heart settle in Your sovereignty. Let my thoughts quiet under the weight of Your Word. I don't need to strive when You've already secured the outcome. Your peace is my pillow. Your promises are my protection.

I declare that I rest in fulfillment. You are not a man that You should lie. Your Word will not return void. I lay down in confidence, knowing that the same God who spoke the promise is the God who will bring it to completion.

In Jesus' name, Amen.

DAY 20

Release

Freedom for the Wounded Places

> "The Spirit of the Lord is on me, because he has anointed me to preach good news to the poor. He has sent me to heal the broken hearted, to proclaim release to the captives, recovering of sight to the blind, to deliver those who are crushed,
> —Luke 4:18 WEB

Father, this evening I release every wound, every hidden place of brokenness, and every lingering sorrow into Your healing hands. The Spirit of the Lord is upon Jesus, and He came to heal the brokenhearted, to proclaim liberty to the captives, and to set the oppressed free. So I choose not to hold onto pain You've already come to carry. I release what I cannot fix, and I welcome the freedom You give.

Where I've been bound by emotional trauma, confusion, bitterness, or fear—I declare liberty. I let go of the identity formed through pain and step into the wholeness of my calling. You are restoring dignity, peace, and joy in the places where life tried to steal them.

I declare that the chains of yesterday are broken. The wounds of the past are no longer my prison. I am healed and free. I walk into this evening as one who has been set loose by the power of the gospel.

In Jesus' name, Amen.

Renew

Your Word Revives Me

> My son, attend to my words. Turn your ear to my sayings. Let them not depart from your eyes. Keep them in the center of your heart. For they are life to those who find them, and health to their whole body.
> —Proverbs 4:20-22 WEB

Lord, this evening I turn my heart to Your Word, for it is life to those who find it and health to all their flesh. Your words are not empty—they are Spirit and they are life. I open my ears to hear what You are speaking over me. Let Your Word be like medicine to my soul, like rain to dry ground, like light to my path.

I ask You to renew me—physically, emotionally, and spiritually—through the power of Your truth. Let every weary part of me be restored by the breath of Your voice. Let healing flow from Your promises and strength rise from Your presence.

I declare that I am being renewed by divine truth. I do not live by bread alone but by every word that proceeds from Your mouth. I receive fresh vitality, renewed focus, and inner healing as I meditate on Your Word.

In Jesus' name, Amen.

REFOCUS

I Commit and Align

> Commit your deeds to Yahweh, and your plans shall succeed.
> —Proverbs 16:3 WEB

Father, this evening I commit my works, my plans, and my intentions to You. I realign my agenda with heaven's purpose. I release every scattered idea and half-formed goal, and I ask You to establish my thoughts. Let Your clarity flood my mind, and Your direction guide my next step.

I don't want to live according to impulse or pressure—I want to move by divine purpose. Refocus my vision so that I don't waste time chasing what looks good but lacks Your breath. Align my heart with what truly matters, and let everything I put my hands to reflect Your will.

I declare that my evening is grounded in divine clarity. My thoughts are established. My motives are purified. My goals are refined. I commit all things to You, and You will make the way straight before me.

In Jesus' name, Amen.

Rebuild

Restore Me, O God

> Turn us again, God. Cause your face to shine, and we will be saved.
> —Psalms 80:3 WEB

Lord, this evening I lift my voice with the cry of the psalmist: "Restore us, O God; make Your face shine upon us, that we may be saved." I may not know exactly how to fix what's been broken, but I know You are the God who restores. You revive what's been crushed, and You renew what's been diminished.

Rebuild my strength where discouragement has weakened me. Restore my confidence where fear has spoken too loudly. Shine the light of Your presence over every dark place, and let Your favor rest upon me again. I trust You to do what I cannot—to restore the years, repair the ruins, and reignite my joy.

I declare that restoration is not just possible—it is promised. I am being rebuilt in the presence of God. My heart is being revived. My life is being realigned. The light of Your face is upon me, and I will not be the same.

In Jesus' name, Amen.

Rest

1 Enter Peace, Not Pressure

> He enters into peace. They rest in their beds, each one who walks in his uprightness.
> —Isaiah 57:2 WEB

Father, this evening I choose rest—not just for my body, but for my soul. Your Word says the righteous are taken away to be spared from evil, and they enter into peace. While I'm still walking this journey, I receive that peace now—peace from anxiety, from constant striving, and from mental exhaustion. I don't have to carry more than You've asked me to carry.

Let me lie down in stillness, not stress. Let the noise of today fade into the calm of Your presence. Let me remember that Your rest is not a reward for finishing everything—it's a gift of grace for trusting You.

I declare that I will rest in divine peace. My heart is not racing. My thoughts are not scattered. I lie down in calm assurance, confident that the One who watches over me does not sleep or slumber.

In Jesus' name, Amen.

DAY 21

RELEASE

OUT OF DISTRESS, INTO SPACE

> Out of my distress, I called on Yah. Yah answered me with freedom.
> —Psalms 118:5 WEB

Father, this evening I lift my voice from the narrow places—the tight, pressured, and overwhelming corners I've found myself in. I cried out to You in distress, and You answered me by setting me in a broad place. So now, I release every constriction of fear, stress, and anxiety that has wrapped around my heart. I breathe deeply, knowing You are opening up space for peace.

I let go of the weight of what I can't control, the pressure to prove myself, and the fear of being stuck. You have made room for me. You have brought me into expansion, into freedom, into divine possibility. I step out of the box the world tried to place me in and into the wide-open field of Your grace.

I declare that I am free from confinement. I will not be hemmed in by fear, by others' opinions, or by my own limitations. You have delivered me into space and surrounded me with favor. I walk in liberty tonight.

In Jesus' name, Amen.

Renew

Restoring the Years

> I will restore to you the years that the swarming locust has eaten, the great locust, the grasshopper, and the caterpillar, my great army, which I sent among you. You will have plenty to eat, and be satisfied, and will praise the name of Yahweh, your God, who has dealt wondrously with you; and my people will never again be disappointed.
> —Joel 2:25-26 WEB

Lord, this evening I stand before You with confidence, knowing that You are the Restorer of time. You promised to restore the years the locusts have eaten—years of loss, delay, distraction, and despair. And I receive that promise as my own. You are not just giving me back what I lost—You are making it better, richer, and more fruitful.

Renew my hope where dreams were buried. Renew my strength where time seemed wasted. Restore what was drained in the struggle and pour fresh joy into the seasons ahead. You are the God of recompense, and nothing is beyond Your power to revive.

I declare that my years are not lost—they are being restored. What I thought was gone forever will be returned with increase. I will eat in plenty and be satisfied. Shame is leaving, and restoration is arriving.

In Jesus' name, Amen.

Refocus

Approved and Equipped

> Give diligence to present yourself approved by God, a workman who doesn't need to be ashamed, properly handling the Word of Truth.
> —2 Timothy 2:15 WEB

Father, this evening I set my mind back on truth. I refocus my heart and thoughts on Your Word and my assignment. You've called me to present myself to You as one approved—a worker who does not need to be ashamed, rightly handling the Word of truth. I reject every distraction, every unworthy comparison, and every voice of confusion.

Sharpen my focus so I no longer waste time chasing what doesn't align with my calling. Teach me to discern between what is urgent and what is eternal. Purify my motives. Steady my mind. Let me walk in clarity and conviction, so that everything I do honors You.

I declare that I am focused, faithful, and fruitful. I am equipped for every good work, and I live not for applause but for Your approval. My life is aligned with truth, and I walk in integrity and insight.

In Jesus' name, Amen.

Rebuild

Now Is the Appointed Time

> Yahweh says, "In an acceptable time I have answered you, and in a day of salvation I have helped you. I will preserve you, and give you for a covenant of the people, to raise up the land, to make them inherit the desolate heritage,
> —Isaiah 49:8 WEB

Lord, this evening I receive the word of restoration and divine rebuilding. You have declared this as the time of favor and the day of salvation. I don't miss this moment. I don't dismiss this window. Where things once seemed delayed or denied, You are now opening doors of restoration and redemption.

Rebuild the ruins of missed opportunities. Reconstruct the walls of faith that once crumbled in doubt. Restore the favor that once felt lost. Let the appointed time bring acceleration—let it bring alignment. You have not forgotten me. In this sacred evening moment, I agree with heaven: now is the time.

I declare that restoration is not coming—it's here. I step into divine timing, into fresh grace, and into purpose reborn. You are rebuilding what was broken, and I say yes to Your process.

In Jesus' name, Amen.

Rest

Blessed in the Finished Work

> On the seventh day God finished his work which he had done; and he rested on the seventh day from all his work which he had done.
> —Genesis 2:2 WEB

Father, this evening I enter into rest not as a sign of weakness, but as an act of faith. Just as You rested on the seventh day after completing creation, I rest in the finished work of grace. You blessed the day of rest and called it holy. So I receive Your blessing on this evening as I cease from striving and trust in Your sufficiency.

Let me lay aside the need to perform, to prove, or to push beyond Your pace. You are not impressed by exhaustion. You are honored by trust. I rest not because I've done enough—but because You are enough.

I declare that this evening is blessed. My rest is holy, protected, and purposeful. I am refreshed by Your presence and renewed by Your peace. I rest in the finished work of my faithful God.

In Jesus' name, Amen.

DAY 22

RELEASE

BEAUTY FOR MY ASHES

> to provide for those who mourn in Zion, to give to them a garland for ashes, the oil of joy for mourning, the garment of praise for the spirit of heaviness; that they may be called trees of righteousness, the planting of Yahweh, that he may be glorified.
> —Isaiah 61:3 WEB

Father, this evening I come with open hands and an open heart to exchange the ashes of sorrow, loss, and disappointment for the beauty You promised. I release what has burned me—failed plans, broken relationships, unmet expectations, and silent wounds. You do not ask me to fix them, only to surrender them. You give beauty for ashes, the oil of joy for mourning, and a garment of praise for the spirit of heaviness.

I let go of bitterness and make room for joy. I refuse to cling to grief when You offer healing. I trade heaviness for the uplifting presence of Your Spirit. Let the smoke clear so I can see what You're doing anew in my life. Even when I don't understand the fire, I trust in the transformation it brings.

I declare that the ashes will not be the end of my story. You are crafting beauty from every broken place. Joy is rising, praise is breaking through, and hope is being restored. I release the pain, and I receive Your promise.

In Jesus' name, Amen.

RENEW

BORN AGAIN TO A LIVING HOPE

> Blessed be the God and Father of our Lord Jesus Christ, who according to his great mercy caused us to be born again to a living hope through the resurrection of Jesus Christ from the dead,
> —1 Peter 1:3 WEB

Lord, this evening I bless You for the living hope I have through the resurrection of Jesus Christ. Even when life has felt dull or my vision has dimmed, Your mercy renews me. I am not without hope. I am not stuck in cycles of despair. You have given me a hope that lives, breathes, and grows stronger—even in adversity.

Let this living hope ignite fresh expectation within me. Restore my wonder, revive my passion, and renew my anticipation for what's ahead. Let me not live by what I see with natural eyes, but by what You've spoken and promised. This evening, I breathe in Your mercy and exhale every ounce of cynicism and doubt.

I declare that I am being renewed in hope. My past is not my prison. My future is not uncertain—it is blessed. I carry the living hope of Christ, and it fills my heart with strength for tomorrow. In Jesus' name, Amen.

REFOCUS

SEEK AND RETURN

> Seek Yahweh while he may be found. Call on him while he is near. Let the wicked forsake his way, and the unrighteous man his thoughts. Let him return to Yahweh, and he will have mercy on him; and to our God, for he will freely pardon.
> —Isaiah 55:6-7 WEB

Father, this evening I turn my eyes and heart fully back to You. I refocus my thoughts on Your presence, not my problems. Your Word calls me to seek You while You may be found, to call on You while You are near. So I pause now to seek—not out of routine, but with desperation and love. I realign my heart, my decisions, and my desires with Your will.

Where I've drifted, I return. Where I've hesitated, I say yes again. Where my focus has blurred, I now fix my gaze. I choose to forsake my own ways and thoughts and embrace Yours—higher, holier, and far more fulfilling.

I declare that my evening is marked by divine clarity. I will not be tossed by distraction or swallowed in delay. I am focused. I am attentive. I am seeking—and I will find.

In Jesus' name, Amen.

Rebuild

Redemption Has a Name

> The women said to Naomi, "Blessed be Yahweh, who has not left you today without a near kinsman. Let his name be famous in Israel. He shall be to you a restorer of life, and sustain you in your old age, for your daughter-in-law, who loves you, who is better to you than seven sons, has given birth to him."
> —Ruth 4:14-15 WEB

Lord, this evening I thank You for being my Redeemer—the One who restores what I thought was lost forever. Just as You turned Ruth's story from widowhood to legacy, You are rebuilding the story of my life. Where there has been grief, You bring joy. Where there has been barrenness, You bring fruitfulness. Where there has been silence, You speak life again.

You are my Boaz—my covering, my provider, my restorer of name and future. I believe tonight that You are breathing new strength into my bones and writing a new chapter with divine purpose. I receive the healing balm of Your redemption over every wound and every wasted season.

I declare that joy is being rebuilt. Hope is taking root again. You are restoring honor, family, and future. My name is no longer "forsaken"—it is "redeemed."

In Jesus' name, Amen.

Rest

He Never Sleeps—So I Can

> He will not allow your foot to be moved. He who keeps you will not slumber. Behold, he who keeps Israel will neither slumber nor sleep.
> —Psalms 121:3-4 WEB

Father, this evening I rest in the security of Your watchful care. Your Word reminds me that You do not slumber or sleep. While I rest, You remain alert. While I pause, You continue to protect, to guide, and to uphold. You are the Keeper of my soul, and I am safe in Your hands.

I release the need to stay in control. I silence the inner voice that says, "What if?" I rest, not because everything is resolved, but because I trust the One who never grows weary. You are my defender, and You do not miss a thing.

I declare that I am covered, kept, and cradled in perfect peace. I do not need to fear the darkness or dread tomorrow. You're awake, You're working, and I can lie down in confidence.

In Jesus' name, Amen.

DAY 23

RELEASE

SAFE IN THE DAY OF TROUBLE

> Yahweh is good, a stronghold in the day of trouble; and he knows those who take refuge in him.
> —Nahum 1:7 WEB

Father, this evening I release the need to protect myself. You are my refuge and stronghold in the day of trouble. You know those who trust in You—and I am one of them. I release the fear of danger, the anxiety of uncertainty, and the torment of wondering how things will turn out. You are good, and I take refuge in Your goodness.

I don't have to be on edge. I don't have to brace myself for disaster. I can rest because You are shielding me with loving care. You are not surprised by anything I'm facing, and You will not abandon me in it. So I let go of every need to fight battles You've already taken up on my behalf.

I declare that I am covered by the goodness of God. The trouble may rise, but I am hidden in Your presence. I trust You tonight, and I release every burden that is too heavy for me to carry.

In Jesus' name, Amen.

RENEW

DOUBLE FOR MY SHAME

> Instead of your shame you will have double. Instead of dishonor, they will rejoice in their portion. Therefore in their land, they will possess double. Everlasting joy will be to them.
> —Isaiah 61:7 WEB

Lord, this evening I receive Your promise: for every shameful place, You will give double honor. For every confusion, I will rejoice in my portion. I surrender the shame of past failures, the sting of rejection, and the embarrassment of dreams that didn't happen the way I hoped. You are not the God of leftovers—You are the God of overflow.

Let divine renewal wash over every area of loss. Reignite my joy where discouragement dimmed it. Restore beauty where shame once sat. I welcome the exchange You offer—honor instead of humiliation, rejoicing instead of regret, double for my trouble.

I declare that this is my evening of divine reversal. What the enemy meant to shame me with, You are turning into my testimony. I will walk in double—double strength, double favor, double peace.

In Jesus' name, Amen.

Refocus

Seek with All My Heart

> You shall seek me, and find me, when you search for me with all your heart.
> —Jeremiah 29:13 WEB

Father, this evening I center my heart on You. You promised that when I seek You with all my heart, I will find You. So I let go of half-hearted devotions and distracted thoughts. I fix my attention on You again. You are not far—you are near to those who pursue You with love.

I don't want to miss Your voice in the noise of my evening. Tune my ears to hear You. Turn my eyes toward the unseen, and my heart toward what matters. Help me to pursue You—not for blessings alone, but because You are my treasure.

I declare that I am a seeker of God, and I will find Him. My heart is open. My soul is listening. My spirit is engaged. I seek You—and I will not be disappointed.

In Jesus' name, Amen.

Rebuild

Restore My Soul

> He restores my soul. He guides me in the paths of righteousness for his name's sake.
> —Psalms 23:3 WEB

Lord, this evening I come to You not with strength, but with surrender. My soul has felt drained, scattered, and stretched. But You are the Shepherd who restores. You lead me beside still waters and make me lie down in green pastures—not just to rest, but to be rebuilt from within.

Rebuild my inner life—my confidence, my rhythm, my purpose. Take the pieces I don't know how to put together and make something beautiful again. Let Your restoration go deeper than my behavior. Touch the core of who I am and heal me from the inside out.

I declare that my soul is being restored. My spirit is being refreshed. I'm not just being patched—I'm being renewed. I will walk forward with quiet strength and inner wholeness.

In Jesus' name, Amen.

Rest

You Will Lie Down Secure

> You shall be secure, because there is hope. Yes, you shall search, and shall take your rest in safety. Also you shall lie down, and no one shall make you afraid. Yes, many shall court your favor.
> —Job 11:18-19 WEB

Father, this evening I enter into rest with confidence and peace. You said that I will be secure because there is hope. That I will look around and lie down without fear. So I cast off every anxious thought and heavy emotion. I rest because You have secured my future, my heart, and my night.

Let hope arise in me like a soft light in the dark. Let security settle into my bones like a warm blanket. I do not have to stay on guard—You are guarding me. I am not afraid of bad news—I am confident in good promises.

I declare that I will lie down and no one will make me afraid. I sleep in peace, I rise in purpose, and I dwell in divine safety. My hope is in You, and therefore, I rest.

In Jesus' name, Amen.

DAY 24

RELEASE

SUNG OVER WITH LOVE

> Yahweh, your God, is among you, a mighty one who will save. He will rejoice over you with joy. He will calm you in his love. He will rejoice over you with singing.
> —Zephaniah 3:17 WEB

Father, this evening I release every voice that has spoken failure, fear, or condemnation over me. I silence the echoes of criticism, comparison, and self-doubt—and I tune my heart to Yours. You rejoice over me with gladness. You quiet me with Your love. You exult over me with singing. So I let go of the noise, and I rest in Your song.

I release every lie that said I wasn't enough, every memory that made me feel unloved, and every shadow that clouded my worth. Your love is louder than the shame. Your delight drowns out despair. This evening, I surrender to the truth of who I am in You—chosen, cherished, and celebrated.

I declare that I am not overlooked or forgotten. I am held in divine joy. The King of the universe sings over me, and I release the need to be validated by anything less. My heart is quieted, not by answers, but by Your love. In Jesus' name, Amen.

Renew

Revived by Truth

> Yahweh's law is perfect, restoring the soul. Yahweh's testimony is sure, making wise the simple.
> —Psalms 19:7 WEB

Lord, this evening I thank You for the restoring power of Your Word. Your law is perfect, reviving the soul. When I feel weary, unfocused, or drained, I don't need to run to the world—I run to Your truth. It realigns me, cleanses me, and awakens what's been dormant inside me.

Let the ancient words speak new life into me tonight. Let the familiar promises come alive again. Restore my joy. Refresh my thinking. Reignite my reverence for Your voice. I don't want shallow encouragement—I want deep transformation.

I declare that I am being renewed by eternal truth. Your Word is not just instruction—it is healing. It strengthens what's weak and revives what's dry. I rest under its power and rise with new perspective.

In Jesus' name, Amen.

Refocus

Turn My Eyes from Vanity

> Turn my eyes away from looking at worthless things.
> Revive me in your ways.
> —Psalms 119:37 WEB

Father, this evening I ask You to purify my gaze. Turn my eyes from worthless things—those distractions, illusions, and shallow pursuits that drain my energy and blur my purpose. Let me see what matters again. Refocus me so I'm not pulled by vanity but anchored by vision.

Help me to guard the gates of my heart. Remove the subtle idols that promise satisfaction but never deliver. Lift my eyes to eternal things. Make me aware of where my focus has drifted, and bring me back to the center—Your will, Your way, and Your Word.

I declare that I have eyes to see clearly. I'm not wasting emotional energy on the superficial. I'm focused on what fuels my calling, builds my spirit, and glorifies my King.

In Jesus' name, Amen.

Rebuild

The Desert Will Bloom Again

> The wilderness and the dry land will be glad. The desert will rejoice and blossom like a rose. It will blossom abundantly, and rejoice even with joy and singing. Lebanon's glory will be given to it, the excellence of Carmel and Sharon. They will see Yahweh's glory, the excellence of our God.
> —Isaiah 35:1-2 WEB

Lord, this evening I believe You to bring beauty out of barrenness. The wilderness seasons, the dry places, the silent years—they are not wasted. You have declared that the desert will rejoice and blossom like the rose. So I dare to hope again. I dare to believe that fruitfulness is possible even after long droughts.

Rebuild the garden of my soul. Water the seeds of promise buried beneath disappointment. Let joy erupt like wildflowers in a once-barren place. Let praise rise up from the soil of sorrow. You are the God who makes things grow in unexpected places.

I declare that my dry season is not final. New life is sprouting. Hope is budding. Beauty is breaking forth from hard ground. The wilderness will sing again.

In Jesus' name, Amen.

Rest

Strength and Peace Are Mine

> Yahweh will give strength to his people. Yahweh will bless his people with peace.
> —Psalms 29:11 WEB

Father, this evening I rest in the gift of strength and peace. You give strength to Your people—not just for battle, but for balance. And You bless Your people with peace—not just for quiet moments, but for every moment. I receive that blessing now. I breathe it in. I let it wash over every anxious place in my soul.

I don't have to earn peace—I receive it. I don't have to fight for strength—I embrace it. You have already spoken the blessing, and now I agree with it. I lie down in confidence, not because the world is calm, but because You are my calm.

I declare that strength is rising in me and peace is settling on me. I am not afraid of weakness, because You are my portion. I rest in divine quiet, upheld by holy strength.

In Jesus' name, Amen.

DAY 25

RELEASE

HE HEALS THE BROKEN PLACES

> He heals the broken in heart, and binds up their wounds.
> —Psalms 147:3 WEB

Father, this evening I release every wound still lingering in the quiet corners of my heart. I hand You the hidden pain—the disappointments I never voiced, the betrayals I tried to forget, and the cracks that no one sees but You. You are near to the brokenhearted, and You heal every shattered piece. I do not need to hold it together when You are the One who holds me.

I release the pressure to pretend. I release the fear that my brokenness disqualifies me. You are not repelled by my weakness—you draw near to it. You gather every piece and begin the work of restoration, not just to fix, but to make new.

I declare that healing has begun. I am not defined by what broke me, but by the One who is rebuilding me. The pain is no longer my identity. Wholeness is my portion, and hope is my inheritance.

In Jesus' name, Amen.

RENEW

A NEW HEART WITHIN ME

> I will also give you a new heart, and I will put a new spirit within you. I will take away the stony heart out of your flesh, and I will give you a heart of flesh.
> —Ezekiel 36:26 WEB

Lord, this evening I surrender my heart to Your renewing touch. Where my heart has grown tired, cynical, or numb—breathe new life. Take the stony, hardened places and give me a heart of flesh—tender, teachable, and burning again for You. I want to feel deeply, love purely, and believe freely like I once did.

Remove what has crusted over through disappointments. Wash away the residue of bitterness or unbelief. Give me a fresh heart, one that beats in rhythm with Yours. A heart that forgives easily, loves fully, and obeys without hesitation.

I declare that a divine heart exchange is taking place in me. I am not stuck in patterns of apathy or hardness. I am renewed with passion, mercy, and wonder. This is the evening of my heart's transformation.

In Jesus' name, Amen.

Refocus

Remain in Me

> Remain in me, and I in you. As the branch can't bear fruit by itself, unless it remains in the vine, so neither can you, unless you remain in me.
> —John 15:4 WEB

Father, this evening I draw near and re-anchor my life in You. You are the Vine, and I am the branch. Apart from You, I can do nothing. So I release the scattered distractions that have pulled me away, and I return to abiding in You—where fruitfulness flows and peace is sustained.

Teach me not just to visit, but to remain. To live in constant awareness of Your presence. Refocus me on relationship over performance. Let my thoughts stay tethered to Your truth, and my desires aligned with Your will. I don't want busyness without abiding.

I declare that I am rooted, grounded, and connected. My life will bear much fruit because I remain in You. I do not strive to impress—I stay to be transformed.

In Jesus' name, Amen.

Rebuild

Healing and Restoration Declared

> 'Behold, I will bring it health and cure, and I will cure them; and I will reveal to them abundance of peace and truth. I will cause the captivity of Judah and the captivity of Israel to return, and will build them, as at the first.
> —Jeremiah 33:6-7 WEB

Lord, this evening I stand on Your promise to bring health and healing. You declared peace over broken places and restoration over what was devastated. You will rebuild the ruins and cleanse the stains of the past. You're not just mending what was—you're restoring what should have been.

So I lift to You every area of my life that has suffered loss—relationships, years, opportunities, or vision. I declare Your word over them: healing is coming. Restoration is underway. Peace is overtaking chaos. What looked like an ending is becoming a beginning.

I declare that You are the God who rebuilds from ruins. My life is not in decline—it's in divine construction. Health is springing forth. Peace is reigning. Joy is returning.

In Jesus' name, Amen.

Rest

Held by the Hand of God

> For I, Yahweh your God, will hold your right hand, saying to you, 'Don't be afraid. I will help you.'
> —Isaiah 41:13 WEB

Father, this evening I find comfort in the nearness of Your hand. You have said, "I will take hold of your right hand," and I believe it. You are not distant. You are not passive. You are walking with me, holding me, and calming every fear with Your presence.

As I lay down, I release the need to have all the answers. I let go of the fears I haven't voiced, and the stress I haven't shared. You are my Helper, and I don't have to be afraid. You are holding me through the storm, through the silence, and through the stillness.

I declare that I rest in the grip of grace. I am not falling—I am being held. I am not alone—I am protected by the hand of God. Peace is mine, because You are near.

In Jesus' name, Amen.

DAY 26

RELEASE

WHERE THE SPIRIT IS, I'M FREE

> Now the Lord is the Spirit and where the Spirit of the Lord is, there is liberty.
> —2 Corinthians 3:17 WEB

Father, this evening I step into the liberty that only Your Spirit brings. Where Your Spirit is, there is freedom—freedom from fear, freedom from performance, freedom from every yoke that's tried to hold me hostage. I release the chains I've been dragging: the fear of failure, the grip of shame, the weight of trying to prove myself.

I don't belong to bondage—I belong to grace. You didn't save me to live in captivity. You set me free so I could walk with confidence and peace. I shake off every lie that says I'm stuck, and I rise into the liberty that flows from Your presence.

I declare that I am free. I am not bound by the past, not limited by my weakness, and not controlled by fear. The Spirit of the Lord is here—and I live in that freedom.

In Jesus' name, Amen.

Renew

Overflow with Hope

> Now may the God of hope fill you with all joy and peace in believing, that you may abound in hope, in the power of the Holy Spirit.
> —Romans 15:13 WEB

Lord, this evening I receive a fresh infilling of Your hope. You are the God of hope, and You fill me with all joy and peace in believing. Let hope rise in me—not based on what I see, but based on who You are. Let joy overflow where discouragement tried to settle. Let peace flow like a river where stress tried to take root.

You don't just give a little hope—you fill me to overflowing by the power of the Holy Spirit. So renew my heart with confidence. Refresh my mind with promise. Let every doubt be drowned in Your faithful love.

I declare that I am filled tonight—not with fear, but with faith. Not with despair, but with overflowing hope. My cup is not empty—it is running over, because You are my source.

In Jesus' name, Amen.

Refocus

Do Not Love the World

> Don't love the world or the things that are in the world. If anyone loves the world, the Father's love isn't in him. For all that is in the world, the lust of the flesh, the lust of the eyes, and the pride of life, isn't the Father's, but is the world's. The world is passing away with its lusts, but he who does God's will remains forever.
> —1 John 2:15-17 WEB

Father, this evening I turn my eyes away from the distractions and desires that try to pull me from You. Your Word reminds me that the world and its cravings are passing away, but whoever does Your will lives forever. So I realign my heart tonight with eternity. I refocus my affections and desires on things that last.

Strip away the pride, the lust, and the chasing after temporary things. Let me love what You love. Let me live for what really matters. Keep me anchored to the eternal even as I walk through the temporal. Help me to value obedience over applause, and surrender over success.

I declare that I have the mind of Christ. I'm not ruled by the fleeting—I'm anchored in forever. My focus is set. My heart is clear. My life is Yours.

In Jesus' name, Amen.

Rebuild

From Lame to a Remnant

> "In that day," says Yahweh, "I will assemble that which is lame, and I will gather that which is driven away, and that which I have afflicted; and I will make that which was lame a remnant, and that which was cast far off a strong nation: and Yahweh will reign over them on Mount Zion from then on, even forever."
> —Micah 4:6-7 WEB

Lord, this evening I stand in awe of how You gather the broken, the scattered, and the wounded and turn them into a remnant of glory. You take the lame and make them a strong nation. You rebuild what others reject. I am not too damaged for Your use—I am a vessel of redemption.

Rebuild me from the inside out. Use the weak places as the foundation for Your strength. Where I've been limping, give me divine momentum. Where I've been exiled in shame or regret, call me home into restoration and purpose.

I declare that I am being rebuilt—not as I was, but better. You are gathering the remnants of my life and shaping them into something glorious. The rejected are being restored. The broken are being raised.

In Jesus' name, Amen.

Rest

Peace from the God of Peace

> Now the God of peace be with you all. Amen.
> —Romans 15:33 WEB

Father, this evening I receive peace—not just the feeling of calm, but the peace that comes from being in right standing with You. You are the God of peace, and You Yourself bring wholeness into every area of my life. I lay down anxiety, restlessness, and anything that would disrupt the stillness of my soul.

Let Your presence calm every storm inside me. Speak peace over my mind. Whisper rest into my heart. I'm not chasing rest—I'm abiding in it. Your peace guards me, surrounds me, and holds me through the night.

I declare that I rest in wholeness. Nothing missing, nothing broken. My soul is at peace, and my evening is wrapped in the quiet strength of Your love.

In Jesus' name, Amen.

DAY 27

Release

Let Go, Stand Still

> Moses said to the people, "Don't be afraid. Stand still, and see the salvation of Yahweh, which he will work for you today: for the Egyptians whom you have seen today, you shall never see them again. Yahweh will fight for you, and you shall be still."
> —Exodus 14:13-14 WEB

I release the battle, Lord. I release the striving, the panic, the temptation to fix what is beyond me. I declare tonight that I will not be moved by fear, nor ruled by the voices of pressure and defeat. I release every anxious thought that tells me I must act now, speak now, solve now. I choose instead to be still and watch You work. You are fighting for me in ways I cannot see. You go before me with power, and You surround me with peace.

I surrender the impulse to control outcomes and the fear of standing still. You are not limited by time, by people, or by circumstance. When I can't move forward and turning back is not an option, I will not despair—I will trust. You are parting seas I didn't even know existed. You are delivering me, not through force but through faith. And so I pause in holy confidence.

I let go of frantic prayers and receive the quiet assurance that You are already handling it. My fear no longer dictates my response. My heart is aligned with the stillness of heaven. I stand, not in retreat, but in readiness—to see Your glory revealed in my situation.

In Jesus' name, Amen.

Renew

Satisfy Me Again, O God

> Satisfy us in the morning with your loving kindness, that we may rejoice and be glad all our days.
> —Psalms 90:14 WEB

Lord, tonight I ask for something deeper than strength—I ask for satisfaction. I don't want to merely get through the evening; I want to be renewed in the depths of my soul. Satisfy me early with Your steadfast love—even now as this day comes to a close. Pour joy into the places that grew bitter today. Revive the dreams that grew dim. Let Your mercy be more than a concept to me—let it be my daily bread.

I need Your love to lift what stress has crushed. I need Your joy to drown out the sorrow. I ask not just for peace, but for the gladness that comes when I realize I am completely known and completely loved. Teach my heart to rejoice again, not in outcomes, but in intimacy with You. You are enough—You are more than enough.

Tonight, I trade exhaustion for elation. Not because everything went right, but because You are still here. You are still faithful. You are still good. My strength is returning. My heart is lifting. My soul is singing again. Let joy flood me like a river and run over into every space I occupy. In Jesus' name, Amen.

REFOCUS

KEEP THE FIRE BURNING

> not lagging in diligence; fervent in spirit; serving the Lord;
> —Romans 12:11 WEB

Father, I fix my focus on You and fan the flame of my spirit. I refuse to grow lukewarm in the evening hours. Though the day has drained my strength, I stir up my zeal. I am not just a believer—I am a burning one. Renew my passion for You. Reignite the spark of devotion that busyness tried to smother. Let my heart burn again with purpose, with urgency, with holy pursuit.

I will not serve You out of obligation but out of overflowing love. I want to be diligent in spirit, fervent in heart, and relentless in obedience. I resist every distraction that numbs my focus. I lay aside apathy, fatigue, and passivity. I choose to lean in rather than zone out. Let my evening be an altar, not an escape. Let my spirit be alive with the awareness that You are still speaking and still moving.

I declare that the fire in me will not die down with the setting sun. I am committed, fueled, and focused. I will not lose my edge. I fix my eyes on the One who is worthy of it all—and from this place of holy focus, I live and serve with passion.

In Jesus' name, Amen.

Rebuild

Joy Will Be Restored

> I will remove those who grieve about the appointed feasts from you. They are a burden and a reproach to you. Behold, at that time I will deal with all those who afflict you, and I will save those who are lame, and gather those who were driven away. I will give them praise and honor, whose shame has been in all the earth. At that time I will bring you in, and at that time I will gather you; for I will give you honor and praise among all the peoples of the earth, when I restore your fortunes before your eyes, says Yahweh.
> —Zephaniah 3:18-20 WEB

Lord, You are gathering me. You are restoring me. You are rebuilding what sorrow tried to scatter. Tonight, I receive Your promise of restoration—not just of things, but of joy. You are quieting my pain and singing over me with rejoicing. What I thought was lost forever is not beyond Your reach. You are calling me out of shame and into celebration. You are turning my mourning into music.

I bring You every place in my heart that feels forgotten, abandoned, or damaged by the days behind me. You promise to deal with those who oppressed me and to restore what was stolen. I believe it. I speak it. I receive it. Let this evening be a turning point, where restoration begins in my soul. Restore my dignity. Restore my laughter. Restore my expectancy for good again.

I declare that the ruins of yesterday will not define the landscape of my future. What was torn will be mended. What was taken will be returned. And what was once quiet sorrow will become loud rejoicing. You are rebuilding joy in me—and I will dance again. In Jesus' name, Amen.

Rest

COVERED IN BLESSING AND PEACE

> 'Yahweh bless you, and keep you. Yahweh make his face to shine on you, and be gracious to you. Yahweh lift up his face toward you, and give you peace.'
> —Numbers 6:24-26 WEB

Lord, I rest tonight beneath Your blessing. I settle my heart under the covering of Your name. I may not understand every detail of this day, but I am certain of this: You bless and You keep. You shine Your face upon me. You turn toward me with grace. You lift Your countenance over me and give me peace. That is my inheritance, and I receive it fully.

I don't need everything to be figured out to be at rest. I only need to know You are with me. And You are. I rest in the knowledge that I am not forgotten, not forsaken, not exposed to the chaos of life without divine protection. Your peace guards my emotions. Your light steadies my steps. Your name marks me as Yours.

I declare that I am not striving—I am sustained. I am not scattered—I am settled. The blessing of the Lord surrounds me and rests upon me. My soul is covered. My mind is calm. My heart is full. And in this holy covering, I find a peace that cannot be shaken. In Jesus' name, Amen.

DAY 28

RELEASE

LETTING GO, TRUSTING THE PLAN

> For I know the thoughts that I think toward you," says Yahweh, "thoughts of peace, and not of evil, to give you hope and a future.
> —Jeremiah 29:11 WEB

Father, this evening I release my tight grip on what I thought life should look like. I lay down every plan formed in my own understanding, every timeline I've clung to, and every burden I've carried trying to force things into place. Your plans for me are filled with peace and not harm. They are not delayed—they are divine.

I release control and surrender to Your wisdom. I let go of the pressure to perform, the weight of comparison, and the sting of disappointment. You are not late. You are leading. And because Your thoughts are higher, I choose to trust.

I declare that I am not defined by delays or detours. I am aligned with the purposes of heaven. I release what I cannot control and rest in the goodness of the One who holds my future.

In Jesus' name, Amen.

Renew

Strengthened by Everlasting Comfort

> Now our Lord Jesus Christ himself, and God our Father, who loved us and gave us eternal comfort and good hope through grace, comfort your hearts and establish you in every good work and word.
> —2 Thessalonians 2:16-17 WEB

Lord, this evening I open my heart to receive Your encouragement—stronger than any words spoken by man, deeper than any temporary comfort. You have given me eternal hope and grace that strengthens me from the inside out. Even when my heart has grown weary, Your Spirit breathes life back into me.

Renew me, Lord—not just emotionally, but spiritually. Let courage rise where fear lingered. Let joy bubble up where heaviness once sat. You are the God who speaks strength into my soul and infuses my steps with boldness.

I declare that I am not discouraged—I am divinely strengthened. Hope is not fading; it's flourishing. I am renewed by grace and kept by love.

In Jesus' name, Amen.

Refocus

Let Your Love Lead Me

> Cause me to hear your loving kindness in the morning, for I trust in you. Cause me to know the way in which I should walk, for I lift up my soul to you.
> —Psalms 143:8 WEB

Father, this evening I lift my soul to You. Let me hear of Your steadfast love at the close of this day, for I trust in You. Lead me away from distractions, away from weariness, and into clarity. Where I've been unsure of my next step, refocus my heart on Your voice.

Clear the fog of my emotions. Recenter my thoughts on Your goodness. Help me to walk forward not based on pressure, but on peace. You are the Shepherd of my soul, and I choose again to follow Your lead.

I declare that I will not wander in confusion. I hear Your voice behind me saying, "This is the way." I refocus, realign, and move forward in divine direction.

In Jesus' name, Amen.

REBUILD

ARISE AGAIN BY HIS WORD

> Soon afterwards, he went to a city called Nain. Many of his disciples, along with a great multitude, went with him. Now when he came near to the gate of the city, behold, one who was dead was carried out, the only son of his mother, and she was a widow. Many people of the city were with her. When the Lord saw her, he had compassion on her, and said to her, "Don't cry." He came near and touched the coffin, and the bearers stood still. He said, "Young man, I tell you, arise!" He who was dead sat up, and began to speak. And he gave him to his mother.
> —Luke 7:11-15 WEB

Lord, this evening I bring to You every area in my life that feels like it's died—dreams deferred, hope silenced, love lost. Like the widow's son at Nain, there are things I've carried toward the grave. But just as Jesus stepped in and touched what was lifeless, I believe You are stepping in now with resurrection power.

Rebuild what I thought was too far gone. Speak life where there was mourning. I welcome Your interruption—Your voice that says, "Arise." Nothing is beyond Your ability to restore. You bring joy where there were tears and beginnings where there were only endings.

I declare that You are touching the lifeless places. Resurrection is coming. Hope is rising. The procession of grief is turning into a testimony of glory. In Jesus' name, Amen.

Rest

Taste and See His Peace

> Oh taste and see that Yahweh is good. Blessed is the man who takes refuge in him.
> —Psalms 34:8 WEB

Father, this evening I quiet myself in the sweetness of Your presence. You said, "Taste and see that the Lord is good," and I have. Even when life is complex, You are still kind. So I rest not in the perfection of my circumstances but in the perfection of Your nature.

I take a deep breath and receive the peace that flows from knowing You. Your goodness surrounds me. Your presence comforts me. I don't have to figure everything out—I only need to trust that You are near and that You are good.

I declare that I rest in divine delight. I have tasted, and I've seen—my God is good. My heart is safe. My soul is calm. Peace is not far; peace is here.

In Jesus' name, Amen.

DAY 29

RELEASE

FEAR HAS NO HOLD HERE

> Even though I walk through the valley of the shadow of death, I will fear no evil, for you are with me. Your rod and your staff, they comfort me.
> —Psalms 23:4 WEB

Father, this evening I release the fear that has gripped my heart. Even though I walk through the valley of shadows—shadows of uncertainty, of loss, of what-ifs—I will not be afraid. You are with me. Your rod and Your staff, they comfort and guide me. I release the fear of bad news, of failure, of rejection, of tomorrow. They are shadows, not substance. You are my reality.

I let go of every imagined outcome and choose to dwell in Your presence. I release the need to understand everything and embrace the peace that comes from knowing You are near. I will not rehearse fear in my mind—I will remember Your faithfulness.

I declare that fear has no place in me. I walk through valleys with courage because You are my Shepherd. I am not abandoned. I am not alone. I am upheld by the One who never leaves.

In Jesus' name, Amen.

Renew

Quiet Confidence Will Rise Again

> For thus said the Lord Yahweh, the Holy One of Israel, "You will be saved in returning and rest. Your strength will be in quietness and in confidence." You refused,
> —Isaiah 30:15 WEB

Lord, this evening I come back to the stillness of trust. In returning and rest I find strength. In quietness and confidence, I find my renewal. I don't need noise to feel secure. I don't need answers to feel safe. I need You. So I retreat into Your presence—not to escape, but to be rebuilt.

Let the rushing wind of anxiety die down. Let the noise of the day be hushed. Speak peace over the scattered pieces of my thoughts. Renew me not with hype, but with holy calm. Let Your Spirit gently but powerfully restore my core.

I declare that I am being renewed in stillness. My confidence is not in what I do but in who You are. I rise from this moment with inner strength and fresh resolve.

In Jesus' name, Amen.

Refocus

The End Is Better

> Better is the end of a thing than its beginning. The patient
> in spirit is better than the proud in spirit.
> —Ecclesiastes 7:8 WEB

Father, this evening I realign my focus. You said the end of a matter is better than its beginning. I release the need to have it all figured out now and choose to trust the process. What You start, You finish. And even if I don't understand the middle, I know the ending is written in victory.

Help me to let go of frustration with slow progress or delayed answers. Teach me to see through the eyes of eternity. The end You've ordained is filled with purpose, beauty, and fruitfulness. I will not despise small beginnings or unfinished prayers.

I declare that I am not stuck—I'm in process. And the end will testify of Your goodness. I press on with faith, knowing that what's ahead is greater than what's behind.

In Jesus' name, Amen.

Rebuild

Be Restored, Be Made Whole

> Finally, brothers, rejoice. Be perfected, be comforted, be of the same mind, live in peace, and the God of love and peace will be with you.
> —2 Corinthians 13:11 WEB

Lord, this evening I receive the call to be restored. Your Word says to aim for restoration, to encourage one another, and to live in peace. I lay down division, discouragement, and despair, and I ask You to rebuild the places that have been fractured—relationships, hopes, identity, and strength.

Let harmony return where there was conflict. Let clarity come where there was confusion. Let wholeness take root where there was brokenness. You are the God of love and peace, and You dwell where healing is welcomed. So I welcome You into every room of my life.

I declare that restoration is not a wish—it is happening now. I will be made whole, and I will be a vessel of restoration to others. Peace is returning. Joy is rebuilding. God is in my midst.

In Jesus' name, Amen.

Rest

Grace for This Day Only

> Therefore don't be anxious for tomorrow, for tomorrow will be anxious for itself. Each day's own evil is sufficient.
> —Matthew 6:34 WEB

Father, this evening I rest in the grace You've given—for today, not tomorrow. I release the weight of what's next, what's pending, and what's unknown. Tomorrow will come, but with it will come new mercy. So I choose to end this day with peace, not pressure.

Let Your calm settle over me like a blanket. I'm not behind—I'm covered. I'm not failing—I'm held. I've done what I could today, and You are doing what only You can. I lay it down and leave it with You.

I declare that I rest under grace. I will not carry tomorrow's worries into this evening. I sleep in peace because I live in surrender.

In Jesus' name, Amen.

DAY 30

RELEASE

LETTING GO OF VENGEANCE

> Don't seek revenge yourselves, beloved, but give place to God's wrath. For it is written, "Vengeance belongs to me; I will repay, says the Lord."
> —Romans 12:19 WEB

Father, this evening I release the burden of revenge, resentment, and unresolved pain. You have said that vengeance is Yours—you will repay. So I lay down my desire to defend myself, to make others see my pain, or to prove my worth through retaliation. I confess that my heart has carried some weight it wasn't meant to carry—grudges, silent accusations, bitter memories. But now I choose to release it all at Your feet.

You are a just Judge, and I trust You to handle what I cannot. I release the people who wronged me, the situations that wounded me, and the words that lingered long after they were spoken. I give them to You—not because they were right, but because I refuse to let their wrongs rule me.

I declare that I am free from the cycle of vengeance. My hands are clean, my heart is light, and my spirit is rising. You will handle what needs to be handled. I will rest in peace and live in joy.

In Jesus' name, Amen.

RENEW

FULLNESS OF JOY AGAIN

> You will show me the path of life. In your presence is fullness of joy. In your right hand there are pleasures forever more.
> —Psalms 16:11 WEB

Lord, this evening I come to be renewed in Your presence. In You there is fullness of joy, and at Your right hand are pleasures forevermore. I'm not just seeking relief—I'm seeking renewal. Let my joy be restored. Let my soul be refreshed by the beauty of who You are. I come not for things, but for You, the Giver of life and the Restorer of joy.

Every weary place in me is being revived. Where the oil has run low, You are refilling. Where the light has dimmed, You are relighting. You are not a distant God—you are near, and Your nearness is my renewal. I will not settle for shallow happiness. I want deep joy—the kind that sustains and satisfies.

I declare that joy is returning. My spirit is being lifted. My countenance will change because Your presence changes everything. I am renewed from the inside out.

In Jesus' name, Amen.

Refocus

Open the Door of My Heart

> Behold, I stand at the door and knock. If anyone hears my voice and opens the door, then I will come in to him, and will dine with him, and he with me.
> —Revelation 3:20 WEB

Jesus, this evening I realign my heart and focus on the One who knocks. You stand at the door, waiting—not to bring condemnation, but communion. Not judgment, but joy. I open the door wide tonight, not with fear, but with faith. Come in. Be Lord here. Dine with me. Dwell with me. Drive out the distractions that keep me from hearing You clearly.

Refocus my eyes from every idol, every temporary obsession, every anxious pursuit. I don't want to miss You. I don't want to be so busy or bitter that I ignore the knock. You are gentle, but persistent. And this evening, I say yes again.

I declare that my eyes are fixed on You. I will not live distracted. I will not keep the door locked with excuses or pride. You are welcome here. Be glorified in my life.

In Jesus' name, Amen.

REBUILD

TEARS WILL NOT BE WASTED

> He will wipe away every tear from their eyes. Death will be no more; neither will there be mourning, nor crying, nor pain, any more. The first things have passed away."
> —Revelation 21:4 WEB

Father, this evening I lift my heart to You—the One who promises that every tear will be wiped away. You see it all. The hidden pain, the quiet prayers, the silent struggles. And You are not distant from my sorrow. You promise restoration, even from grief. You rebuild not only what was visible, but what was internal. You're healing my heart as You restore my life.

No more death. No more mourning. That's the future You're bringing. And even now, You're beginning it in me. I give You the ruins, the ashes, the wounds—and I trust You to make something beautiful. Rebuild my hope. Rebuild my expectations. Rebuild my belief that joy can live here again.

I declare that sorrow will not have the last word. You are the God who rebuilds what was broken. My tears are not wasted. My future is secure. You will make all things new.

In Jesus' name, Amen.

Rest

Kept From Falling

[God] is able to keep [you] from stumbling, and to present you faultless before the presence of his glory in great joy,
—Jude 1:24 WEB

Lord, this evening I rest in Your keeping power. You are able to keep me from stumbling, from slipping into despair, from giving up too soon. When my strength wavers, Yours does not. When my grip loosens, You hold on tighter. I don't have to perform to be preserved—I just have to rest in You.

You are faithful to finish what You start. And I believe You're still working on me. So I refuse to fear the fall. I won't live with dread. I won't end this day in anxiety. You are able to present me blameless, covered in grace, filled with peace.

I declare that I rest secure in Your hands. My stability is not found in perfection, but in Your power. You are my Keeper, and I sleep in peace, knowing I am held and kept.

In Jesus' name, Amen.

Epilogue

The Evening Still Belongs to God

You've made it to the end of *Command Your Evening*—thirty days of prophetic prayers, declarations, and moments of divine alignment. That is no small journey. Every evening you showed up—tired or refreshed, burdened or joyful—you made the choice to speak life over your hours, to release what weighed you down, to renew your strength in the Lord, to refocus on what matters, to rebuild what was broken, and to enter God's rest.

But this isn't the end. It's a beginning.

This book was never meant to be a finish line, but a foundation. These thirty days were your training ground, your spiritual reset, your evening revival. Now, the challenge is to carry what God has started into your everyday rhythm. Make commanding your evening a lifestyle, not just a devotional habit. Let the prayers you've spoken shape the atmosphere of your home, your relationships, and your heart.

You've learned to resist the drift. To reject spiritual passivity. To take hold of the hours between work and sleep and fill them with faith, truth, and intentional surrender. Don't let that go. Keep showing up. Keep praying boldly. Keep pressing into God as the sun sets and trust that He is still working, even in the quiet hours.

And remember this: when you command your evening, you're not just ending your day—you're preparing your tomorrow.

Stay ready. Stay rooted. And never stop commanding your evening.

In Jesus' name, Amen.

ENCOURAGE OTHERS WITH YOUR STORY

If this prayer guide has strengthened your faith, deepened your intercession, or helped you stand in the gap for our nation, would you consider leaving a short review on Amazon? Your feedback not only encourages others but also helps more believers discover this resource and join in the prayer movement. Every review—just a few sentences—makes a difference and helps spread the call to command the evening. Thank you for being part of this movement.

More from PrayerScripts

COMMAND YOUR MORNING: 30 Days of Prayers and Declarations to Seize Your Day and Shape Your Destiny

There is a battle over every morning—and every believer must choose to either drift into the day or command it.

Command Your Morning: 30 Days of Prayers and Declarations to Seize Your Day and Shape Your Destiny is a spiritually charged guide to help you start each day with purpose, power, and prophetic clarity. This is more than a devotional—it's a call to action. Each day in this 30-day journey is built around **five core biblical themes** that set the spiritual tone for your day: **Praise, Purpose, Protection, Provision** and **Position**. Don't just wake up. Command your morning—and shape your destiny.

COMMAND YOUR NIGHT: 30 Days of Prayers and Declarations to Secure Your Rest and Shape Your Tomorrow

---

Every night is a spiritual battlefield—what you do before you sleep can determine the course of your tomorrow.

Command Your Night: 30 Days of Prayers and Declarations to Secure Your Rest and Shape Your Tomorrow is a powerful devotional prayer manual designed to help you end each day in victory, not vulnerability. Whether you're battling anxiety, spiritual attacks, restlessness, or simply longing for deeper peace, this book equips you to reclaim your night with bold, Scripture-rooted prayers. Each night is structured around five strategic prayer themes: *Shut, Shield, Silence, Show, Sleep.*

SCRIPTURES & PRAYERS FOR DELIVERANCE FROM TROUBLE: 40 DAYS OF PRAYER FOR WHEN LIFE FEELS OVERWHELMING

Are you walking through a season where life feels heavy, hope feels distant, and your prayers feel weak?

Scriptures & Prayers for Deliverance from Trouble is a 40-day journey of honest prayers and powerful Scriptures to help you find peace, strength, and healing when life is overwhelming. Each day offers a personal, Scripture-based prayer written in the language of real faith and raw trust. This devotional isn't about perfect words— it's about real connection with God when you need Him most.

Scriptures & Prayers for Deliverance from Evil:

50 Days of Prayer to Overcome Darkness and Find God's Protection

When darkness presses in, how do you pray?

When fear grips your heart or unseen battles rage around you, you need more than generic words—you need Scripture, truth, and the steady hand of God to lead you through.

Scriptures & Prayers for Deliverance from Evil: 50 Days of Prayer to Overcome Darkness and Find God's Protection is a powerful devotional journey designed to help you pray boldly and biblically through seasons of spiritual warfare, oppression, fear, or uncertainty.

SCRIPTURES & PRAYERS FOR ENGAGING THE ENEMY:

70 DAYS OF PRAYER TO REBUKE THE ENEMY AND RELEASE GOD'S POWER

You weren't called to run from the battle—

you were anointed to win it.

Scriptures & Prayers for Engaging the Enemy: 70 Days of Prayer to Rebuke the Enemy and Release God's Power is a bold devotional for believers who are ready to rise, resist, and reclaim what the enemy has tried to steal. If you're tired of feeling spiritually outnumbered, this book will equip you to fight back—with Scripture in your mouth and power in your prayers. Over 70 days, you'll be guided through five strategic phases of spiritual warfare: (1) Rebuking the Enemy, (2) Releasing Terror Upon the Enemy (3) Praying for the Fall of the Enemy (4) Treading Upon the Enemy (5) When Heaven Strikes.

The war is real. But so is your victory.

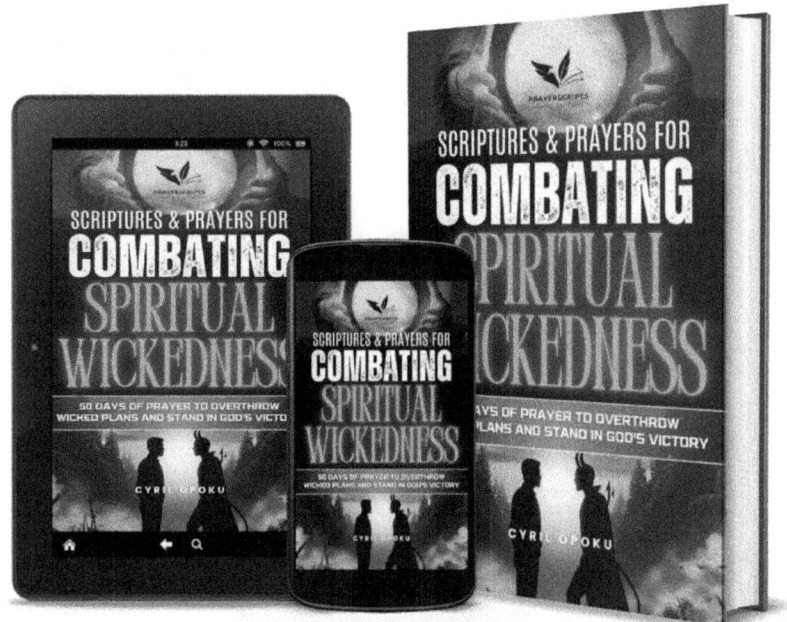

SCRIPTURES & PRAYERS FOR COMBATING SPIRITUAL WICKEDNESS:

50 DAYS OF PRAYER TO OVERTHROW WICKED PLANS AND STAND IN GOD'S VICTORY

Are you facing opposition that feels deeper than the natural? Do you sense hidden resistance working against your progress, peace, or purpose? You're not imagining it—and you're not powerless.

Rooted in the authority of Scripture and fueled by bold, targeted prayers, *Scriptures & Prayers for Combating Spiritual Wickedness* equips you to confront darkness head-on. Each day features a focused Bible passage and a heartfelt, Scripture-based prayer designed to nullify ungodly counsel, disrupt demonic schemes, and establish God's victory in every area of your life.

STANDING IN THE GAP FOR COVENANT AWAKENING:

30 DAYS OF PRAYER FOR NATIONAL REPENTANCE, RIGHTEOUS LEADERSHIP & GOD'S SOVEREIGN RULE

What if your prayers could help turn the tide of a nation?

America stands at a spiritual crossroads. Division deepens, truth is under siege, and righteousness is being redefined. But God is still searching for those who will stand in the gap—intercessors who will cry out for mercy, justice, and national awakening.

Standing in the Gap for Covenant Awakening is a 30-day prayer guide for believers who sense the urgency of the hour and long to see their nation return to God.

STANDING IN THE GAP FOR DIVINE DEFENSE:

30 DAYS OF PRAYER FOR NATIONAL GUIDANCE, GUARDING & GLORY

When the foundations of a nation feel as if they're shaking, prayer is the strongest fortress you can build.

Standing in the Gap for Divine Defense: 30 Days of Prayer for National Guidance, Guarding & Glory is your call to action—a 30-day journey of powerful, Scripture-rooted intercession that invites everyday believers to become watchmen on the walls for their nation. Drawing on timeless truths from God's Word, this devotional equips you to stand in the gap for your nation and **Seek Heaven's Wisdom, Secure Divine Protection,** and **Ignite Spiritual Awakening.** If you sense the urgency of the hour and long to see your country guided and guarded by the hand of God, open these pages. Stand in the gap. Watch Him move.

STANDING IN THE GAP FOR NATIONAL HEALING:

40 DAYS OF PRAYER FOR RECONCILIATION, RIGHTEOUSNESS, AND RESTORATION

What if your prayers could help heal a nation? What if God is waiting for someone—like you—to stand in the gap?

Standing in the Gap for National Healing: 40 Days of Prayer for Reconciliation, Righteousness, and Restoration is a bold, Spirit-filled call to action for believers who refuse to sit on the sidelines while their nation drifts further from God. In a time marked by division, confusion, and moral decline, this book equips you to pray with power, precision, and unshakable hope. Inside, you'll find 40 days of Scripture-based intercession divided into three strategic sections: **Peace, Unity & Reconciliation, Morality, Truth & Righteous Leadership**, and **National Restoration & Reformation**. It's time to stop watching history unfold—and start shaping it in prayer.

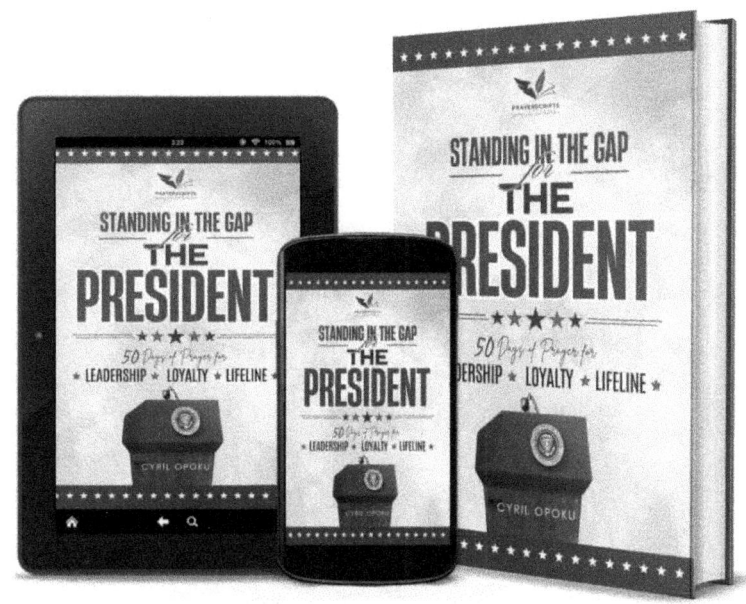

STANDING IN THE GAP FOR THE PRESIDENT:

50 DAYS OF PRAYER FOR LEADERSHIP, LOYALTY, AND LIFELINE

When a nation's leader is under spiritual siege, will you answer the call to stand in the gap?

Standing in the Gap for The President: 50 Days of Prayer for Leadership, Loyalty, and Lifeline is a bold, Scripture-saturated prayer guide for those who understand that the battles facing our leaders are more than political—they are spiritual. Assassination attempts, betrayal from within, and attacks on character and conscience are not just headlines—they're signs of the times. Inside, you'll find 50 days of strategic intercession divided into three high-impact sections: **Presidential Character & Leadership**, **Against Disloyal Insiders**, and **Against Assassination Attempts**. The future of a nation can shift through the prayers of the faithful. It's time to stand in the gap.

www.ingramcontent.com/pod-product-compliance
Lightning Source LLC
Chambersburg PA
CBHW070659100426
42735CB00039B/2337